HOW TO GET
GULF JOBS

HOW TO GET
GULF JOBS

Authored By,

Rajen Maheshwari

Disclaimer

This book has been published with all reasonable efforts taken to make the material error-free after the consent of the author. This book is sold subject to the condition that it shall not, by way of trade or otherwise, be lent, resold, or otherwise circulated without the copyright owner's prior written consent in any form of binding or cover other than that in which it is published and without a similar condition including this condition being imposed on the subsequent purchaser and without limiting the rights under copyright reserved above, no part of this publication maybe reproduced, stored in or introduced into a retrieval system or transmitted in any form or by any other means without the permission of the copyright owner.

Registered Office- 907-Sneh Nagar, Sapna Sangeeta Road, Agrasen Square, Indore – 452001 (M.P.), India

Website: http://www.wingspublication.com

Email: mybook@wingspublication.com

First Published by WINGS PUBLICATION 2024

Copyright © Rajen Maheshwari

Title : How To Get Gulf Jobs

Price : Rs. 599 | $ 15 | AED 50

All Rights Reserved.

ISBN : 978-93-6006-514-0

LIMITS OF LIABILITY/DISCLAIMER OF WARRANTY

Dedication

I dedicate this book to my wife Prafulla Maheshwari. Without her support, inspiration and continuous follow up, it would have not been possible to finish my first dream book.

Acknowledgements

This book is my life journey and the persons who shaped me from rough stone to polished diamond are following. I would like to thank them all at this moment.

My grandmother with whom I passed my child hood and nourished me with love and support and my grandfather who in spite of poverty had small library of religious books like Mahabharat, Ramayana, Amar charitra, Okha haran etc and inspired me to read. He was known as bhagat (religious person) and was leader of our street.

My father Dr Lalit Chandra who inspired me to study hard and become good human being. He was follower of Dr. Ambedkar and Gautam Buddha and was not believing without thinking so he inspired me to think scientifically. He taught us how to live disciplined life. His habit of diary writing I liked very much and still following. His 24 by 7 service to patient inspired me a lot. He earned respect by hard dedicated work and lived life of ideal doctor.

My Mother Shantaben who wished for me to go to gulf to make some good fortune and after her demise due to cancer, I could go to gulf. She shaped my life by taking life changing decisions when I was child. At that time there was no parent teacher meeting in village school. While going for grinding wheat to flour mill with big container on head she will stand in front of school and ask my teacher how is my study. Teacher replied he is studying well don't worry. That was my parent teacher meeting.

My Uncle Saresh Bhai, who was a student of arts college in Rajpipla was bringing novels by Gujarati writers for reading. I used to read very fast, and I finished it in one sitting. So, he cultivated habit of reading books. Reading is the first step of book writing. He wanted to become a writer in the Guajarati film industry and wrote two novels in Gujarati but, due to poor conditions, could not publish them. His hand writing was so clear and artistic that it was looking like printed one.

My ex-boss Mr. Dushyant Chhaya and Mr. Ashok Joshipura who gave us training on how to work in professional life with confidence and face higher management. They gave us full power in decision-making independently, and if any adverse consequences were there, they stood by us.

And finally, my coach Dr Kailash Pinjani who coached me step by step how to write book and how to work on book project with discipline and timeline. I had a dream of writing book but how and what are the steps of book writing I learnt from him. Weekly Friday meetings were very helpful tips in my book writing project.

Preface

With the exploration of large quantities of oil and gas in the gulf and the development of oil and gas-related industries, refineries, and petrochemicals, it became an attractive destination for skilled and unskilled manpower from South-Asian countries like India, Pakistan, Bangladesh, Nepal and the Philippines and other nationalities due to higher tax-free salary and large job opportunity.

Saudi Arabia is the largest producer of oil in the world. Saudi Arabia has about ⅕ of the total oil reserves of the world. About 10 Million barrels of oil are produced per day; with the increase in oil prices, the rain of dollars is pouring into Saudi Arabia. Many multinational oil companies from America, Europe, and Asia work in Saudi Arabia in collaboration with local oil company. Huge industrial development needs technically trained manpower, and India and other neighbouring countries are supplying the majority of its requirements of technical and non-technical manpower. Today @ 1.6 million Indians are staying in Saudi Arabia. About 5.5 million Indians are staying in Gulf countries, with the majority in Saudi Arabia and UAE. Many Saudi companies visit Delhi, Mumbai, Vadodara, Chennai, Kolkata, and other cities of India regularly and recruit Indians through manpower-supplying companies. If anyone has experience with refinery, petrochemical, fertilizer, power plant, or medical or hotel field etc in India, there is a majority chance of getting selected for gulf jobs. Indian NRIs sent 90 billion USD, the highest remittance in the world, in 2022 and that shows the economic power of Indian diaspora.

There is a tremendous magnetic attraction for Indian engineers, technicians, doctors and nurses to get jobs in the Gulf due to 3 to 4 times Indian salary that is too tax-free income. I saw it when I went to G complex on deputation and went to visit one temple on the seashore along with other fellow engineer friends. One friend was sleeping straight on the ground and praying to God to help him to get a good job in the oil and gas sector in Saudi Arabia. Qatar, Oman, UAE, and Kuwait are the countries, engineers wish to go to. Kuwait and Qatar are the most preferred countries as they offer a good pay package. Money is the main driving force behind the migration of manpower around the world.

After arriving in Saudi Arabia, many Indians initially find it difficult to adjust due to culture shock. My friend D was working at my same petrochemical co. in Gujarat as an operator. When he got an offer from a company in KSA Al

Jubail, he was very happy as there were three friends who got selected together as operators for the same gulf company. They decided and distributed responsibility for who would bring utensils, snacks, and some required food items. After staying in a furnished apartment at AL Jubail, his friends decided to move in a cheaper home in a nearby area, and they left him alone. At the office, he was kept on a rotating shift after one week, so he was like an alien in a group of Arabic local operators. Initially, the Arabic language was difficult to understand. Moreover, after coming to KSA, he was suffering from malaria, so his supervisor asked him to take one week's leave and take rest at home to stay isolated. Malaria is considered a contagious disease in the gulf.

Due to all these initial difficulties, at one time, he was under tremendous stress and started thinking about going back to India, as in such conditions, everybody gets initial culture shocks. For him, it was like in English saying, "Difficulties come in battalion". He was having sleepless nights. When we asked him why he was sitting on the sofa at midnight, he told us he was not able to sleep and remembering his family. He cannot forget his family and younger children and wants to go back. It causes culture shock when an expatriate enters the Gulf countries due to large differences in social, religious, and environmental conditions and different food habits.

Fortunately, he was a friend of my colleague U, who joined with me in the same company, and we were staying in the same room. He came from Rabigh, and I came from Yanbu, so we had prior Saudi experience, so it was very easy for us to settle at Al Jubail. Al Jubail was considered better place than Yanbu and Rabigh due to more expats living there so it was like moving to better place. D used to visit my friend and tell him his miseries. U tried to convince him, but he could not. Then he gave up and asked me to convince him to be a senior person. I asked him what the problem was. D replied, "See, my friends left me alone, and I cannot pay a furnished flat rent of 3000 SR per month". Moreover, he is on shift where he works with Arabic operators, and nobody speaks English; they all always talk in Arabic. During the day, nobody was there to talk with him as the majority of apartments were general shift engineers and operators. He has younger children, and he misses them a lot, so he wants to go back and join the same company at G complex, as his boss, the plant manager, is very good by nature, and he has good relations with him. Fortunately, I was also from the same petrochemical co. in Gujarat, India, from where he was coming, and I knew his boss also as he was my 1984 management trainee batch mate.

I explained to him that when he had already landed here in the gulf, it would be very bad on his part to go back just in a few days. Everybody will laugh at him. Moreover, his ex-boss is very good person, but it is not all in his hands to take him back. In private companies, it is the HR department that dictates and decides the policy of recruitment. Many instances have occurred where the boss recommends, but the HR department gives the opposite opinion and employees were not taken back in service. Some times during exit interview employee gives reason of leaving company due to bad HR policies which are viewed negatively by HR while considering for taking back.

I requested him to stay for only three months on a trial basis with us in our room so that he does not need to pay a hefty room rent and then decide on further action. Finally, he agreed to stay for a three-month timeline. Whenever I see him, I always ask how he is feeling now. He was replying he is getting strength by seeing people like us how to survive here. Now, he is settled in Petrochemical Co. in Kuwait happily. He knows more Arabic language than we do because he is in close contact with Arabic operators; slowly, he started understanding a few words and then started speaking Arabic also.

Smoking is the best way to make local friends in the gulf. He was smoking with Arabic operators and making easy friends by offering cigarettes. Now he likes the gulf of course, with money gain and confidence to survive. So, the initial three to six months is like passing through a post weld heat treatment cycle of metal, controlled heating, soaking and cooling. Metal becomes strong after heat treatment, the stress relieving process and so is the human too if he stays for three to six months, he starts liking new place and people.

When one leaves the family and starts living a lonely life, it gives heavy shock mentally and it takes time to heal. Also, the culture shock, and environmental condition of KSA makes the situation worse, but now I heard rapid changes are visible under the new era. Still I miss Saudi Arabia for its world best road conditions and dal foul and tameez (crispy roti) and Saudi friends.

When I came to Bahrain from Saudi in 2010, I met another Indian friend named S. I told him I came from Saudi Arabia, and he told his story that he was offered a superintendent position at a refinery in Yanbu, but he came back to India within three days as he felt it was very difficult to settle. He could not survive there anymore and came back within 3 days. When I was in Yanbu, I saw One operator also joined Yanbu From India, but I saw him weeping like a child to go back home, and with his mother's serious illness reason, he could leave KSA forever.

Then I thought I must write about the Gulf experience and guide my fellow young Indians to think and prepare mentally before coming, also when already landed, not to make hasty decisions and go back instantly. Good chances are not coming again and again. After all, you only decided to come to the Gulf seeing other friends getting more money in the Gulf, so stay for a minimum of three four months and then decide to go back. One of my friends told me that to stay in the Gulf, you must have a strong affinity for money.

Money is the main driving force in the world that causes manpower to flow from lower income to higher income. In last centuries Arabs were coming to India as businessmen and merchants selling Arabian horses and for jobs in the small kingdoms as a soldier. Now Indians are migrating to gulf for jobs and business. Nobody likes to move unless forced. If my public sector company had not been privatized by the government, I would not have moved to Saudi Arabia, and this book might not have been published!!!!!!

India is the largest technical manpower source in the world, producing about one million engineers per year and gulf being the largest oil and gas producing area, needs technically skilled experienced manpower, so synergy exists between two regions: The Middle east and India. It is like made for each other. India imports oil and gas from the gulf and in return exports food items, vegetables and manpower.

Technical and medical manpower from India is going to flow towards the gulf till its oil reserves last. One of my Saudi friends confessed to me that his country is run by Indians. Everywhere from household to construction workers, industrial workers and shopkeepers, drivers, nurses, doctors, engineers, technicians, masons, painters, electricians, plumbers, car mechanics, AC mechanics, merchants, and businessmen, all are Indians. Indian has become a brand name in the gulf, and behind it, many Indians' hard work and dedication lie in its foundation. When Iran oil minister visited my ex petrochemicals company, his remarks after plant visit was, I am happy to see that complete plant is run by Indians only. In the gulf, plants are run by multi nationalities expats and locals. One of my Arabic friends told me Indians are like oxygen; they are everywhere. Kerala is the leading state from where most people have migrated to the Gulf. Even radio channels in Bahrain broadcast in Malayalam and Hindi. Hindi, Tamil, Malayalam movies are shown in local cinemas.

The aim of this book is to guide all expatriates, especially young engineers, operators and technicians, doctors and nurses who aspire to come into the oil and gas field and medical field so that they go with a clear vision, mission and purpose and don't get frustrated after landing in the Gulf. Good and bad people exist everywhere in the world, so the gulf is not an exception. Fortunately, I met many of the best local Arabic friends in the gulf, and they gave me a lot of love, support and respect, which, even I did not receive in India after serving 22 years in a company.

If one expatriate will get inspiration to move to the gulf fully prepared with a positive mind set, high spirits and positive attitude for a better life after reading this book, I will believe my objective of writing this book is achieved.

Regards,

Rajen Maheshwari
B46, Shreekunj Greens,
Opp. Pratham Vatika, Nr. Shreenath Bunglows,
New Alkapuri, Gotri, Vadodara 390021, Gujarat, India.
Phone (M) 0091-9998002315, Bahrain 973-37395075
Email: rajenmaheshwari@yahoo.com
9-11-2024

Contents

Chapter

1

How to Start Searching Job

How to prepare self for Gulf jobs

Positive mindset is very much required to go to the gulf. For that one has to prepare for gulf and experiment whether he can live alone or not. Take every five-year change of job or go for short term deputation to another part of the country. In the first step, remain away from family by attending short deputations to other locations and train yourself to survive alone without family so that initial jerk and, disturbance, culture shock, will be less.

I prepared myself by going on a deputation to another complex of my company. Whenever any requirement arises, I was the first person to apply for deputation. That way I went to N complex, G complex, J complex, on deputation for three months, one month and two months respectively. It gave me the opportunity to work with other complex employees, different food, different culture and language people. Also adjusting with new food habits has increased my self confidence level. It widened my networking and friend circle.

3C means knowledge of car, cooking and computer also must for gulf jobs. In the gulf roads are right hand drive so driver seat comes on left side whereas in India it is left hand drive so driver seat comes on right side. Cooking is also essential as in the gulf you may not get home taste in the restaurants as they are either Arabic, Malayali or Pakistani. so, to get home taste you must learn cooking at home prior to moving to gulf. Computer has become essential tool in office and home. So, without basic computer knowledge it's difficult to survive.

 Lots of networking and working with other than routine friends added many more dimensions to my experience. At N complex I learned a few words of Marathi. Daily going for morning walks with friends and evening walks to N village and jungle road, experienced heavy rain of Raigad district. Going to the company guest house during holidays in Mumbai and coming back by company bus was a very good experience. While walking on the road during the monsoon, I saw snakes, crabs, and other creatures around.

I also got appreciation from other complex management, so I thought if I could work in a different location in India, why I cannot work in the gulf?

How to prepare a CV

There are many websites now that generate CVs for you. A two-page CV is more popular than a lengthy CV that difficult to read. Recruiting agencies and HR companies now search based on keywords from job descriptions. Like if an engineer with experience in the crude distillation unit CDU plant of refinery needs to be recruited, then HR will search for CVs for key word CDU and only pick those CVs which contain the "CDU" word. The CV must contain the words which are required in the advertisement. If the requirement is for a fertilizer plant and you have experience in refinery or petrochemicals, there are less chances to get selected even though everybody knows that the function of a mechanical engineer in refinery, fertilizer or petrochemicals industry remains the same. For chemical engineer or process engineer that flexibility is not there as he has to operate that plant and operation of one plant differs from another.

For example, I had a background in a petrochemical plant, but I had shut-down deputation experience at the world's largest refinery in India, in the FCCU plant, and that helped me to get job of mechanical engineer for the FCCU complex in the Gulf.

How to apply for jobs

First you can attend walk-in interviews which are regularly held at manpower recruitment agents at Mumbai, Vadodara, Chennai, etc. places. I got two companies offer letters through attending interviews at the recruitment agents office at Vadodara and Mumbai. Third offer I received thru email from one agent as I registered on one of leading recruitment agent's portal.

The second way is either to register with these agents on their websites or to apply on the oil and gas sector major companies' websites against advertisements.

The third way is sending CVs to friends who are already in the Gulf and serving in oil and gas sector companies in the Gulf. I arranged a friend's job in my company as my company had a policy to give some incentive if I refer to my friend's CV and he gets selected in an interview and joins the job. This was a win-win situation where the employee gets an incentive and the company gets an experienced employee.

Now there are many platforms like You can post your CV on social media like LinkedIn and Naukrigulf.com etc. manpower recruitment agents' websites.

Which are the websites of companies

You can search on the internet for advertisement. There are many but most of are manpower recruitment companies concentrated in Bombay and New Delhi.

1.   Oil and gas companies of gulf countries

2.   EPC contractor companies working in the Gulf

3.   Manpower recruitment companies working for gulf

Who are the recruitment agents?

In Mumbai there are many recruitment agents who are official agents of major oil and gas companies of gulf.

Some agents only recruit for short term shut-down jobs only. Following list is to indicate some agents but it is not a full list. There are many manpower agents in India following are examples only.

1. Jerry Varghese

2. Gheewala

How to face interview

The best way to learn to face job interviews is to attend as many walk-in interviews as possible. This will remove your fear of the interview, and next time, you will prepare more from lessons learnt from the previous interview. Also, there will be many candidates appearing for interview and from them you can get latest updates of job opportunities.

Read JD job description what is required for the job and know from all sources what skill is required to perform those requirements. Like for stationery equipment engineer you must have pressure vessel design code ASME section VIII div.1 code knowledge and software like PV elite operating knowledge. Likewise, for planning engineers you must have software Primavera knowledge and experience of working in the planning section of an oil and gas company.

Networking to get jobs

Now this is the age of networking. Network is your net worth.

If you have contacts you can do anything and everything. Working in large companies in India gives this networking power as many engineers of these companies are working in gulf and they are so much trusted that just reading the experience of those companies' names in CV itself makes selection easier.

One friend gets jobs for other friends and the domino effect starts. Some time it happened that a complete batch of operators from one company joined the gulf company together. Indians have become brand ambassadors of those companies from where they migrate.

After Indians like Sundar Pichai and Satya Nadella became CEOs of Google and Microsoft in the USA, the Indian image worldwide has gone up. Moreover, Rishi Sunak became prime minister of the UK. If, in the election, 2024, Vice President Kamala Harris would have become president of the USA, it would be the peak for the Indian diaspora to prove that we don't only produce CEOs; we can produce PMs and presidents too. When we had farewell party of H Patel at Bahrain as he got green card and migrating with family at USA, I had given lecture and wished him that from his next generation some body will become president of America. Audience gave good applause to it.

I heard from one of my friends that from his company many engineers were leaving jobs for gulf so the HR department proposed to their CEO that let us have some negotiation with those engineers by offering higher pay and promotions. The CEO replied "Let them go, no negotiations please. They are our brand ambassadors."

Newspaper advertisement

In those days of 2006, the Wednesday edition of Times of India -Ascent was a major source of Gulf job advertisements. Now, social media is very strong to get jobs. Regular visits to LinkedIn, manpower recruitment agents, and company websites and other media provides ample information on recruitment. Networking with friends who are already in the gulf can help in getting recruitment advertisements.

How to manage interview and job

Generally, interviews are being held on Sunday in all metro cities of India so if you are working in a general shift it will not be difficult to attend the interview.

If coming from outside of metro cities now every city is connected with rail and air so it's difficult but not impossible. And remember NO pain NO gain.

I used to travel by night train from Vadodara to Mumbai on Saturday. Attend an interview in the morning and come back by night train on Sunday to Vadodara and resume duty on Monday morning. This was monotonous and sometimes disheartening also but kept on trying and one day got the first offer from Jerry Varghese Vadodara office interview only.

Fraud of recruitment agents

It is very dangerous for new candidates to check whether an agent is a fraud or a real one. Many agents give you lucrative offer by phone call that they have contacts in good company and will get your interview done by keeping your profile in the premium candidate list, bypassing the normal route. But you have to pay some dollars or rupees, and the candidate gets ready to pay. As soon as the candidate agrees to pay, he sends one link for online payment. When he pays, he gets no response, and suddenly, nobody lifts his phone. Finally, he finds that after payment, the agent disappears, there is no proof of payment because all payment was made online and through some link which, once paid, disappears.

Some agents give offers on the letterhead of major multinational oil and gas companies and ask to pay some money for further processing. One of my friends got an offer on the letterhead of a big multinational company for a job in Nigeria Africa. He was very happy and showed us without an interview he got this offer. I told him no multinational company would give you an offer without an interview. This is a fraud; check with their embassy in India. Then he realized that it was a fraud. Remember, major oil and gas companies never charge money from candidates. They pay agents one monthly salary of an employee as a commission once that candidate reaches the gulf and resumes his job.

One day, I got an email from a Canadian company and set up an interview online. After online interview, they sent an offer letter with a good salary and perks. I got attracted to that offer, but I had friends in Canada, too. I told them to enquire and found that the company was not there. It was a fraudulent company, and after checking the website, it was found to be a cheating company. Maybe they will ask for a fee for processing and then disappear. So, based on feedback from friends, I put a full stop on it.

So, in a nutshell if agents ask money please don't pay and try with standard agents only. If in doubt, find out, search on the website and it will reveal the history of that agent company.

For lower-level labour, job agents charge heavy fees for job offers and visas. Labourers take loans to fulfil these charges at heavy interest rates. Labour are hired at very low rates, and when they land in Gulf countries, they find that their salary is not sufficient to send money home and repay loan due to food and other charges. He feels confused about how to survive, send money to family, and repay loans, and he finds no direction on how to get free from this vicious cycle. Then, he starts thinking negatively, which leads to suicide. So do proper homework and contact your friend circle and enquire how much salary is required to fulfil requirements and if you get sufficient salary then only come to gulf otherwise you yourself put in miserable condition.

Chapter

2

FAQ

1. **What are the charges by agents?**

Good company agents do not charge anything from candidates. Yes, they charge a one-month salary from the hiring company. Once a candidate reaches the destination of the hiring company and joins the duty, agent will get one salary of that employee as a commission.

2. **What is the time between the interview and getting the appointment order?**

This varies between different companies. If they require it immediately then also the medical and visa process and resignation needs a minimum of two to three months. One should not resign from his company until a work visa and ticket are received from the agent.

Also, it happened to my friend that he got an offer from Malaysia and then he received a message from the hiring company that due to reduction in oil price his employment is delayed and they will contact when it is required. Still he has not received any message.

3.   Is travelling charge reimbursed for interviews?

Yes, sometimes standard companies pay for travel charges, but in walk-in interviews, generally, they don't pay. If you are shortlisted by a hiring agent, they will negotiate with the interviewing company and provide travel charges. For walk in interview generally they don't pay.

4.   Are Medical test charges reimbursed by the company?

Yes, a good company reimburse all medical charges done before joining the company. Now they have made a GAMCA gulf medical centre's association so candidates once failed in one centre cannot get passed from another. Earlier there was no coordination and candidates used to take a medical test from another destination if failed in one destination.

5.   What is the salary range for engineers in the Gulf?

It varies from private to public or government company. It ranges from about 2000 to 5000 BHD PM. plus house rent allowance and travel allowance are paid additionally. Some companies provide free medical for self and family.

Western expat is getting special allowance plus free furnished housing. So western employee gets almost double the salary than his counterpart Indian employee.

6.   What are the visa types and their charges?

Generally, for work in the Gulf, you need a work visa, that is arranged by the hiring company; also, an engineer's registration in local government offices is required for practising as an engineer. In Bahrain, it is called COPP, issued by the council for regulating the practice of engineering professions. In government company, company arrange to get this license, but in private company, it is the employees' responsibility to get this license.

There are single visa and family visa. In Single visa case employee has to bear visa fee and travel charges for family by his own whereas in case of family visa company provides visa fee and travel charges for family.

There are many types of visas in Saudi Arabia, like entry-exit visas, final exit visas, and multiple entry visas. Nowadays, many changes have come up in Saudi Arabia. For family members, 40 BHD per month, are charged for dependents. Many employees have sent their families back to India due to this additional financial burden.

7.   **What is the difference between a contract and a direct hire employee?**

Direct hire employees are on the payroll of the main company and he gets more respect and salary. He gets job security and bonus and more leave and company benefits. He cannot be removed easily and the company has to serve notice period before removing him.

Whereas contract employees are supplied thru manpower supply company. He is an employee of a contract company through whom he is hired by the main company. He is hired by a PO purchase order and needs to be renewed. He can be removed by the next day as the owner company manager has to make one phone call only to the business development manager BDM of the agent company to remove him.

The only benefit in a contract company is if an employee is removed from one company, the contract company will try to depute him to another company where its employee has gone on vacation or found some alternate job for him.

One of my friends spent around two years doing different company jobs through a contract company. He was even given the job of administration officer in a contract company office handling visas, tickets, iqama, and documentation work for other employees.

Initially I also joined a manpower supply company in Saudi Arabia through which I was deputed in a petrochemical company of Saudi Arabia. Company was very good and was owned by one of the princes of Saudi Arabia. If we resign, the company will give a full settlement and exit visa and don't harass the employee, so its reputation was very good. Even the doctor who took my medical exam exclaimed, saying Prince A is your sponsor.!!!

However, there were some contract companies which were harassing employees and would not give final exit visas but sent them back through exit re-entry visas so that they cannot come back again, and salary also will not pay full if employee resign.

8. Which are the most searched websites by expats in the Gulf?

The most searched site is the currency exchange rate site because every month's salary day, the exchange rate is the first question. Earlier, there used to be long queues for transferring money, as in Saudi Arabia, there were very few money exchanges centres. But in Bahrain, there are many centres. The only problem was we could not withdraw more than some BD per day, so we had to collect it on a daily basis and, with cash, go to exchange centres.

Now, all these hassles are over, and we can transfer online. Also, if we have an SBI account in India and Bahrain, we can transfer it without any remittance charge. Now, online transfer is more popular because it involves just playing with fingers on a mobile phone, and money gets deposited into our Indian account. Long ques have become past now.

The second site search is job search sites. Many expats come to the Gulf, whichever company they get first, and then try to switch over from one company to another by application and job interview. From manpower supply company or contract employee to direct company hired employee. Also, they don't allow job transfers in the same country sometime, so we have to try other countries. When I was selected for another company in Saudi Arabia, the agent asked me how I would go there as I already work there and job transfer is not allowed. I Said I have proof of your company email, and when I saw the proof, he believed it. Email message was circulating in expats that this rule is not applicable now. Third site is expatriate.com for buying and selling second hand furniture and cars by expats.

The fourth site is the return air flight ticket prices from the Gulf to India and back. If you book early, you get a lower price, but if you book on holidays and festival days like Eid, it is the highest. Now, air tickets price has become so volatile that in the morning, they will show one price, and in the evening, they will show another price.

The airline website also sometimes plays with ticket prices, so if you search from one computer the second time you open for booking on the same computer, the price will be higher, or the price will be shown less, but booking will not be allowed, and when you go for booking after some time the price will be higher. I have experienced this, as I was travelling almost every 3 months during living alone. Some airlines are so professional that they don't give even free water in the flight. that is also chargeable. Extra charges are adding up day by day for window seat, legroom seat, food, luggage, flexible dates, cancellation etc. It looks air lines will charge for oxygen also we breath in the plane in future!

9. **Which country has the maximum movement of expats in the gulf?**

Saudi Arabia is more dynamic that way as people keep on coming and going fast in Saudi. Going on a short vacation is also an indication that he is going for an interview. I also whenever going to India tried to club more and more interviews at Bombay.

If somebody sends his family back and puts an advertisement to sell his car, then it is a strong indication that he is leaving the country or changing his job. Household item-selling advertisements on expatriates.com are the second indication.

10. How was oil discovered, and when?

Oil was first discovered in 1932 in Bahrain in the Gulf. Bahrain was ruled by the British at that time and was managed from India by the British. Also, no major method was developed for finding the location of oil wells. Generally, it is said that where calcium silicate rock structures are found, there is a possibility of oil under the earth. So, the discovery team was from an American company that had arrived for this job. Initially, all crude produced was exported to America by ship. Then, a small refinery of 10000 barrels per day was commissioned in Bahrain in 1936.

In Saudi Arabia, the story was somewhat different. Government invited major oil companies for exploration. The same American company from Bahrain went there as Saudi Arabia, which was just 18 km away from Bahrain. They went by ship from Bahrain to Saudi Arabia. They discovered some oil in the first well. After that, they spud more wells but didn't succeed. Then, one clever mind thought to spud deeper into the well from which they found some oil. They spud deeper, and then oil started flowing from the oil well in early March 1938 from a depth of approximately 1450 meters and then the rest is the history.

The company township at Dhahran is considered the best in Saudi Arabia. It has all the facilities of a modern township, so employees from all nationalities and all corners of the world can stay with family and work peacefully. Now, Saudi Arabia has @20% of the world's total oil reserves.

Today Saudi Arabia is the strongest economy in the gulf due to the highest oil production.

11. How were people travelling to the gulf when planes were not invented?

In old times when planes were not there, people used to travel from one country to another by land or ship route. Western people were travelling from London to Basra by bus and from Basra to Bahrain by ship. It is worth noting that from London to Kolkata the bus was plying taking 50 days of travel crossing many countries which was called hippie route and a distance of 16000 km. Until 1976 it was in service.

12. Which are the liberal countries in the gulf?

Oman, Bahrain and UAE etc. are liberal countries which allow all religions prayer places to build and worship.

Church, temple and Gurudwara exist in these countries. Now in Abu Dhabi a big Hindu temple was recently built by the BAPS organization. In Bahrain, the king has donated land to build a temple on it at Salmabad area and in the near future it will be reality.

Recently there was SOM yagna ceremony at the place of temple and thousands of Indians were gathered there and performed their religious puja. Daily, different Indian states performed bhajans and drama from their state. It was a unique program in Bahrain, my friend S was in the executive committee of this yagna committee. We attended two-day program as our friends took part in it.

Prime minister of India Mr. Narendra Modi's visit to the gulf countries helped in getting land for temples. Abu Dhabi temple is one example where he openly thanked the ruler of UAE for giving land for the temple.

13. Are Good quality Schools available in the Gulf?

In many cities in the Gulf, Indian embassies manage Indian schools. They are following a central school CBSE course. Indian schools now attract local students very much as they also consider the Indian school CBSE syllabus to be the best. In Bahrain Indian school Each standard class is from A to Z, and about 13000 students are studying in an Indian school. It is the largest expatriate school in the Gulf was established in 1950.

When I went to Yanbu it was a small city and had no Indian school. Children of Indian expats were studying in American schools and companies were paying school fees. American school fees were very high, it was an added benefit to expats as per my Indian friend.

Now other private schools are also operating in the gulf. In Bahrain, New millennium school is there which has DPS school syllabus and fees are higher than Indian schools.

14. Are there any risks of salary reduction in the Gulf?

Generally, salaries are not reduced as that is fixed. Bonuses may vary according to company profit, so some companies give 2 to 3 bonuses per management decision. Salary is also affected by the currency exchange rate, so it can affect Indian income if the rate goes down in the Gulf currency or the US dollar. The US dollar has a fixed currency rate of exchange with gulf currencies, so it remains constant. For example, In Bahrain it is 1BHD equal to 2.65957 USD.

I experienced a salary reduction of 20 per cent when it was reduced from 12 to 10 Indian rupees INR per Saudi riyal SAR when I was in Yanbu in 2007. Some smart engineers do not transfer money to India and keep it in gulf in dollars or local currency. Now the dollar price has doubled, so automatically, rupees also doubled. Yes, there are risks also in keeping all money in a foreign land. In case of war or unforeseen reason, if we have to leave the country urgently, it becomes difficult to transfer all the money. Also, there is a risk of remittance tax.

Overtime makes a big difference in the salary of employees in the gulf. Some companies give overtime liberally and ask employees to do overtime as per their workload mainly in projects. Some companies are very strict and do not give overtime at all instead give compensatory off in lieu of extra work done so that is also a variable factor.

When I was in Yanbu in 2007, some of the employees of my Indian company came there for a new petrochemical company project. They were doing a lot of overtime as it was a project. Every Friday Saturday they go to office. In project and shutdown jobs, there are possibilities of overtime.

15. What about promotion and increment?

Promotions are very limited in the gulf so the best way to get a promotion is to change the job at the interval of every 5 years when you get another better opportunity. Salary increase is directly proportional to the number of jumps you do from one company to another. It will give double benefit like change in company culture, country and with higher salary. Initially six months to one year will be settlement time in new company as we have to learn new policy, procedures and standards.

Increment is also based on individual performance and that is based on rating given by management. If your performance is rated EXCELLENT you get a maximum increment, if your performance is VERY GOOD you get medium increment and if you have a GOOD rating you get normal increment. POOR rating results in job loss also.

16. Which are frequently used Arabic words?

- Ahlan wa sahlan means Well come

- Sukran means Thank you

- Salam walaikum means peace be upon you.

- In response, you have to say "walekum salam", which means upon you be peace.

- Kaif Al haal means, how are you?

- Al hamdulillah means praise be to God.

- Insha Allah means God willing

- Mashallah means what God has willed, for surprise

- Sabah Al khair means good morning. In response, you have to say Sabah Al Noor, good morning

- Sakhbarak (for men) means what is new with you (Sakhbarech for women)

- Shlonak means what you are doing?

- Zain means good

- Khalaas means finished

- Khalli Walli means take it easy or don't worry

- Bismillah by the name of God. When in Saudi, I brought a cake in my farewell party and started cutting it. My Saudi friend said I should say "Bismillah" and then cut, and I did it.

- Mohamed is the largest name in the world, you can ask anybody by Mohamed if you don't know the name of the person in the gulf. Also, a friend who has to show nearness will call "Abu Mohamed" to his near friend or Abu with son or daughter's I was calling my friend U as Abu suhani.

- Yella Yella means quick quick.

- Kullu tamam means all is good or all is well

- Habibi means my dear

- Mohandees means Engineer

- Tabib means doctor

- LA means NO and Aiwa means Yes

17. What are the Arabic numbers?

(i) Wahid means one

(ii) Itnin means two

(iii) Talata means three

(iv) Arba means four

(v) Khamsa means five

(vi) Saba means six

(vii) Sitta means seven

(viii) Tamania means eight

(ix) Tisa means nine

(x) Asra means ten

(xi) Miya means hundred

18. Is there scope for women engineers in the Gulf?

Yes, in some liberal countries like Bahrain UAE and Kuwait etc there are chances for women engineers also. In Bahrain, in my company there were local and expat women engineers working with us. Some expat couples also work.

19. How about foreign tours and overtime?

Some of the companies are liberal to send expat for foreign deputation for technical work like FEED and detailed engineering stage of project or for working in EPC company offices abroad, technical discussion or material inspection for the project. Similarly, some departments like shut-down and project gives sufficient overtime to complete shut-down and project in time as if it delays will result in production loss and revenue loss. Per day delay cost million dollar as project cost are in billion dollars.

20. What are the best strategies for mechanical engineers to go to the gulf?

Fresh Mechanical engineers should gain experience from oil and gas or petrochemical companies in India for five years after graduating. Then, he should move to a multinational EPC company in India as a rotating engineer, static engineer, piping engineer, planning engineer etc., for five years to obtain specialization in one field. Then, he should move to the Gulf, work in an oil and gas company for 10 years, and finally land in Canada, USA, Australia, or other European countries for a better life for himself and future generations.

America and Canada have so much resources and less population compared to India that it will last for another 500 years without any problem.

This way, he can maximize his opportunities and maintain a balance between money and a better life style. He can give citizenship of developed countries to his children with education in the world's best universities. He can purchase a house and car after moving to developed countries. He can survive without a job there for one year. I have seen many Indians coming back to the Gulf after getting passports from Canada, the UK, and the USA and earning double the salary of their Indian friends. Canadian passport holder can work in USA so many of my friend of ex company are working in USA now after getting Canadian passport. Huston USA is major location for oil and gas field jobs. Many petrochemicals company and oil refineries are situated there.

21. Which things are missed by Indians when they are abroad?

Many things are missed by Indians like friends, relatives, seasons, fruits, good and bad incidents when they could not remain present due to vacation issues.

Rainy seasons are also missed by Indians in the Gulf because sometimes, one day of rain in India is equivalent to seasons of rain in the Gulf. Vegetables and fruits like mangoes are missed, and festivals like Makar Sankranti (kite festival) of Gujarat, where all the people of my city of Vadodara will be on the rooftop and flying kites only full day with music, sweets and crackers, are missed. Festivals of lights (Diwali celebration), festivals of colours (Holi celebration), Ganesh Chaturthi celebration, etc., are missed. When our near and dear relatives and friend die in India and we could not go to attend their funeral it feels very bad. When we fall sick in gulf country it feels like let us go back. Everybody wants to die in their motherland.

22. How I could manage culture shock in Saudi Arabia?

I could manage culture shock due to the following reasons. I lived in a mixed society and studied in a Muslim school in Hansot district, Bharuch, Gujarat so I had some basic knowledge of Islam. In my life journey I lived a rural life where no basic amenities of today's world like TV, Car, refrigerator, sofa, dining table, or bathroom were available. Every four years, we had draught conditions, and we had little to eat. Sometimes my grandmother used to cook rice soup. We had farms and cattle like bullocks and cows. I have also travelled in a bullock cart. Generally, for the marriage, we used to travel to another village by bullock cart. I spent my childhood in mango orchards and agricultural farm work. I could not study in one place due to the transferrable job of my father as a doctor and non-availability of better schools. So, every four to five years, I changed my school. All this made me strong and prepared me to adapt to change of new places. So, when I landed in Saudi, I decided to face any condition whatsoever come in a life journey like purna and Buddha story.

I lived rural village life in my childhood, small town life during study and city life during job at Vadodara and now gulf life, lived all age like bullock cart age, cycle age, scooter age, bike age, car age, SUV age, BMW age, TV age, computer age, mobile age, internet age, and now AI age.

When I joined the first company in Vadodara in 1984 there was no computer in office. All drawings were made on drawing boards by draughtsmen/mechanical designers and all communication were through IOM inter office memo and physical letter and files. Getting type written things were like luxury.

All this stage made me strong to live in any situation without complain.

23. How can we become global citizen?

Now a days it is time of globalization and nobody can make progress just living in his own city, state or country and staying in one company life time. He has to move outside for better education, jobs and better life. I have seen many families whose children are staying in different countries like USA, Canada, Australia and parents in India.

We can become global citizen by thinking in balanced and broad way. Think all religions are equal and respect for them. All people are good if we are good and doesn't discriminate based on their colour, caste, creed, religion, gender, geography, state, country and look. Doesn't discriminate because one eats non vegetarian food or drink alcohol. Try to adopt good thing from all religion and culture and leave bad thing from own. Try to adopt food and learn local language and enjoy local festivals. Do like romans when you are in Rome. My Dutch friend gave very good answer when I asked him which religion he follows. he replied I try to become a good human being. When I said I believe in principle of Buddha my Saudi friend told me we consider him as one of the prophets. Sometime educated Indians also don't hesitate to ask caste of fellow Indians in abroad!! Knowing that caste is positive factor for few but negative factor for many.

24. How can we remove silo thinking?

We can remove silo thinking by seeing full picture of life cycle. Initially when we joined public sector petrochemicals company in Vadodara, we never thought that we will change the job as it was feeling like we got golden job. We were suffering from best company, best city Vadodara syndrome. We will retire from Vadodara that was the mindset.

We lost many opportunities due to this short sightedness. Now I think if we had opted for N complex, we would have landed in gulf much earlier age due to its location in jungle and proximity to Mumbai to attend walk in interviews. We could have moved to Canada after passing 10 years at gulf and become Canadian citizen now. Then we did not opt for G complex also considering same syndrome. We could have left the job after 5 years at G complex and got many offers due to mega project experience. We did not change to EPC company which were new and were opening branches in Vadodara and wanted to recruit experienced engineers from refinery and petrochemicals industry in Vadodara. When I left at the age of 46 it was too late, as age increases possibility of getting job in gulf decreases. I was denied direct hire employee job at Yanbu due to my age as management set maximum age limit as 45 years, even though had excellent performance.

Chapter

3

Education

What qualifications are required for Gulf jobs?

For oil and gas field engineering graduates in chemical, mechanical, instrumentation, metallurgy, civil, electrical, environment, fire, diploma engineering and BSc for operator and technician job, BSc for lab technician jobs. BSc Geology for geologist job.

For building construction graduation in civil, structural, and architectural.

for medical job MBBS and post-graduation in any branch. BSc Nursing for nursing job.

BDS for dental job B. physio. for physiotherapist, B. pharm for pharmacist, MBA hospital management, for hospital administrator job. BE IT or Computer science for IT jobs.

BSc/MSc science, maths, BA BEd, BA music, PhD for teachers' and professors' job

Hotel management for hotel industry. CA/MBA Finance for banking jobs.

What are the main fields and posts for which manpower is required?

Oil and gas technical field jobs,

Various job for the chemical/mechanical/instrument/ electrical/metallurgy field are available. These lists are only for examples and are not complete. In the upstream, steel, dairy, and other sectors, there may be many new jobs and titles coming up, so the latest jobs you may find on job portals, company websites, advertisements and on social media like LinkedIn. In various companies the Personnel department is renamed as human resource department (HRD), and now human capital management HCM.

1.	Operator

2.	Chemist

3.	Lab technician

4.	Process Engineer, Process specialist

5.	Operation Specialist

6.	Hazop engineer

7.	PSSR engineer

8.	RCM engineer

9.	Production Engineer

10.	P&U engineer

11.	Technician engineer

12.	Safety engineer

13. Energy engineer

14. Mechanical engineer

15. Maintenance Engineer

16. Planning Engineer

17. Design Engineer

18. Project engineer

19. Rotating equipment engineer

20. Fixed equipment engineer, stationary equipment/ static equipment engineer

21. Pump engineer

22. Stress engineer

23. HVAC Engineer

24. Utility engineer

25. Workshop engineer

26. Refractory specialist

27. Paint specialist

28. Coating specialist

29. Commissioning Engineer

30. Piping supervisor

31. Piping engineer

32.   Construction Supervisor

33.   Lead engineer

34.   Structural supervisor

35.   Field Engineer

36.   Instrument engineer

37.   Analyzer engineer

38.   Fire and gas engineer

39.   Reliability Engineer

40.   Tank engineer

41.   Electrical engineer

42.   Civil -structural engineer

43.   Building engineer

44.   Shut-down engineer

45.   Shut-down planning engineer

46.   Shut-down superintendent

47.   QC inspectors

48.   QC engineers

49.   Thickness gauging technicians

50.   Radiography technicians

51.   Heater specialist

52. Documentation engineer

53. AutoCAD designer for mechanical, civil, electrical and instruments

54. 3D modelling designer

55. Major special engineer (major special project)

56. Area engineer

57. Mechanical maintenance engineer

58. RIK engineer (replacement in kind equipment engineer)

59. HR Specialist

60. Finance officer

61. Safety officers

62. Job watchers

63. Insulation technicians

64. AC technicians

65. Western recruitment officer

66. Eastern recruitment officer

67. Employee experience officer

68. Risk manager

69. PMO manager

70. Environment engineer

71.   Incident investigation engineer

72.   Data analyst

73.   IT help desk engineer

Construction sector jobs

1.   Civil engineer

2.   Architect

3.   Structural engineer

4.   HVAC Engineer

5.   Mason

6.   Carpenter

7.   Tiles fitter

8.   Plumber

9.   Ac mechanic

10.   Welder

11.   Aluminium window makers

12.   Steel grill and gate makers

13.   Horticulturist

14.   Gardeners

15.   Bar benders

16.   JCB operator

17.   Crane operator

18.   Heavy truck drivers

19.   Cleaners

20.   Sofa makers

21.   Furniture makers

22.   Car painter

23.   Car Drivers

24.   Bus drivers

25.   Helpers

26.   Painters

27.   Scaffolders

Medical field jobs

1.   Doctors

2.   Consultants

3.   Nurses (Male/Female)

4.   Radiologist

5.   Surgeon

6.   Ophthalmologist

7.   Gynaecologist

8.   Orthopaedics

9.   Child specialist

10.   Dermatologist

11.   Physicians

12.   Pharmacist

13.   Physiotherapist

14.   Dentist

15.   Psychiatrist

16.   X-Ray technician

17.   Hygienist

18.   Dietician

19.   Cleaners

20.   Receptionist

Hotel management field

1.   Receptionist

2.   Cook

3.   Helper

4.   Stewards

5.   Bartender

6.   Musicians

7.   Singers

8.   Dancers

9.   Belly dancers

10.   Guitarist

11.   Ghazal singers

12.   DJ player

13.   Coffee maker

14.   Restaurant manager

15.   Purchase manager

Malls and restaurants, bars, etc.

1.   Desk clerk/cashiers

2.   Cook

3.   Manager

4.   Sales girls and sales boys

5.   Cleaners

6.   Coffee makers

7.   Singers and dancers

Travel sector jobs

1.   Booking agent

2.   Visa officer

3.   Liaison officer

Aviation Sector

1. Pilot

2. Air hostess

3. Ground staff

4. Loader/drivers

5. Customer agent

Education field

1. Teachers

2. Principal

3. Music teacher

4. PT teacher

5. Lab Assistant

6. Clerks

7. Minibus/bus drivers

Fertilizer, Steel, cement and power plant

There are fertilizer plants, steel plants and cement plants in the Gulf, and many Indians are working in the Gulf based on experience from Indian plants. In Saudi Al Jubail, there is one steel plant, and I met one engineer who was working in India in one of steel plant who was staying in my building and was working in Al Jubail steel plant. Similarly, one

Indian cement company has a cement plant in Bahrain, and this brand is very popular locally.

How many years of experience is required?

A minimum of 5 to 10 years of experience is required. Sometimes freshers also start searching for jobs in the Gulf, but all companies want experienced employees as they have to show how many employee years of experience they have in the company. This might impact insurance premiums, so the majority of companies will not take freshers. They have to start their journey from a company of oil and gas, like a refinery, petrochemicals, or fertilizer, engineering, procurement, and construction EPC company. Another reason for not recruitment of fresh engineers in gulf is to provide local fresh engineers a job and associate him with experienced expats so that after 5 years local can take full responsibly and expat can be replaced.

Experience of which company is essential?

For technical fields, engineers from refinery, petrochemical, oil exploration, fertilizer, steel manufacturing, power plants, desalination plants, chemical plants, contractor company involved in piping fabrication and erection, quality control company, third party inspection company etc.

For the medical relevant field of specialization or MBBS, pharmacy, hospital management Nursing, Dental, physiotherapy etc. in gulf MBBS doctor can do practice.

Additional qualification required?

Software skills using different engineering software like Primavera for planning engineer, SAP for maintenance engineer, Caesar II for piping stress engineer, SAP PM and PMP for project engineer, API ASME certification for QC inspectors, NEBOSH certification for safety engineers, RMP for risk managers etc. In many good companies Obtaining a higher degree is encouraged and one promotion or increment is awarded to encourage enhancement of skill and knowledge of employees.

What additional general knowledge information desired?

Knowing the history, geography, religion and culture, crime rate and climate of the country, location from India you are going to etc. will help in getting confidence because many countries in Africa have low security and sometimes, we feel that it was the wrong decision to migrate there.

When my friends went to Nigeria from my Indian company, they were abducted by mafias and then released after payment of ransom money by the company which they joined. Later, they came to know that there is an arrangement between kidnappers and companies. When my friend joined duty, company itself give telephone number which to dial if kidnapped.

Also, another friend told me that when he went to Nigeria for job and stayed at a hotel many phone calls came from unidentified persons that sir you called a car for the airport, your car is ready at ground floor waiting for you please come down. My friend said he didn't ask but to trap him, they do this type of talk and if somebody comes down, he will be kidnapped. One of my friend had bad experience of loosing money in Dare salaam.

For gulf, Knowledge of Islam, knowledge of Arabic language and 3C i.e. car, computer and cooking will make your life easy. Knowledge of Rules and regulations of the country is also helpful.

Try to see the geography and history of the country you are going to. also study the food and culture of the country you are going to.

Any country has their culture and customs, and if you don't follow them, it's difficult to get settled there. Like in Saudi Arabia, if you burp loudly, releasing gas from your mouth is not considered a good habit. Like in India, if you drink water in an open public area during Ramadan is prohibited in gulf, and if you do, it is a punishable offence. Many people were deported due to this mistake. Poppy seeds are not allowed in the Gulf, but they are widely used in India as a spice for making veg and nonveg curry thicker, and if you are found carrying them at the airport in the Gulf, it may put you in serious offence imprisonment. Poppy seeds are considered a drug in the gulf.

I had studied at a Muslim school at Hansot District Bharuch in Gujarat, India, where my father was working as a doctor in a primary health centre (PHC). It was very helpful in my gulf job as I had a basic knowledge of Islam. I had my Muslim friends and used to go to their homes. During the Eid festival, I was eating biryani with them, going to Eidgah Maidan where horse running competition was arranged. I attended my friend's relatives' last rites at the graveyard. From that time, I knew the five pillars of Islam: Roza, Namaz, Zakat, Shahada, and Hajj. In Hansot I observed unity of Muslims as sarpanch was mostly elected from Muslim community though population was 50:50. Also liked their system of helping poor family from zakat. One time, my arabic friend told me, you have good knowledge about Islam.

Does an American and European degree and passport have any impact on salary?

Yes, if you are a UK, USA, or European passport holder and have an American, UK, or European degree, your salary will be almost double, and promotion will be faster. It has high respect in the gulf. Many Indians come in their thirties with experience and money in the gulf, move to Canada, return with a Canadian passport, and get double salary. Likewise, many Pakistan origin take a degree from the UK and come to the Gulf and get a good salary, position and respect.

One Indian expat had mentioned his address as UK but his passport was Indian. HR officer told him that if he get UK passport his salary will be double.. He inquired for it and found minimum six months required to get UK passport. he directly wrote letter to UK ex PM Margaret Thacher that if he is given UK passport he will bring all money to UK and UK's economy will improve. She recommended for it and he got UK passport in one month time with double salary.

One of my bosses in Saudi Arabia had an American degree and passport and came to the gulf. He had gained high respect and control. His parents migrated from India Gujarat to Karachi Pakistan during 1947 separation. Then from Pakistan he migrated to the USA and got higher degrees and came to the gulf. He was talking with me in Gujarati language as we had common mother tongue.

Is knowledge of English required?

Yes, the official language used by companies and government offices is English. Indians have an advantage over the Chinese is our knowledge of English, due to which Indians could spread all over the world so rapidly especially in the common wealth countries.

Many local people in gulf countries don't know English. In Saudi Arabia, police, drivers and local vendors don't know English, so we had to learn some Arabic words like alatool, which means go straight, Mafi kalam, Mafi Arabic means I don't know Arabic language, khalas, etc. Fortunately, my first flat partner, S, knew Arabic in KSA as initially, he stayed with Lebanese people in a labour camp where he learned Arabic.

Does a degree certificate need to be authenticated by the government and embassy?

Yes, it is required to be stamped by the Indian government and foreign country embassy where you are moving for jobs. Now agents are doing this job. earlier in my time in 2006, we had to personally go to new Delhi to get it stamped from the ministry of external affairs, ministry of human resource department, and the Saudi embassy to get it stamped.

In case of difficulties, do we get any help from the Indian embassy?

Yes, in many cases the Indian embassy helps its nationals. For various certificates like marriage certificate, affidavit, notarized document etc. embassy is providing services. Always get registered with embassy and have phone number of Indian embassies in your diary.

I was travelling from Mumbai to Vadodara by train after leaving my brother-in-law at Mumbai airport. We saw some people seated in front of me, and their faces looked unhappy. I asked them where they were coming from. They said they came from Saudi Arabia, and the agent cheated them. They were embroidery tailors and making ladies' dresses in Vadodara. The agent told them to go to Saudi Arabia to make good fortune and they got attracted and paid heavy fees for visas and tickets. When they landed in Saudi Arabia, they were sent to the desert for goat and sheep rearing job, which they refused to do. So, the owner of the cattle farm kafil lodged a complaint of theft against them, and they were arrested and put in jail. They were beaten by police and put in a cell which was not fit for sleeping. After some days, they were released and walked on the road of Jeddah, weeping as they had nothing in hand, no passport and no money. In Saudi Arabia, a passport is held by the employer of company in his custody. When one Pakistani car driver saw them weeping, he asked what happened. They narrated all the incidents. He said I will take you to the Indian embassy and complain there, they will help you. They went to the embassy and complained. The embassy gave them shelter and arranged a temporary passport, visa and ticket, and also provided food for some days.

In times of disturbances, the Indian embassy helps evacuate Indian citizens. There are films also on real incidents. We saw the film AIR LIFT in Bahrain. This film was about a real incident that happened in Kuwait when Iraqi president Saddam Hussein attacked and captured Kuwait. How did all Indian citizens go to Amman, Jordan, from Kuwait by road as Kuwait airport was captured by Iraqi army. From Jordan, Air India lifted Indians from Amman and sent them to Delhi safely. Recently, many Indians, along with other nationalities, were shifted from Yemen to India by ship sent by the Indian government due to the war between the Houthis of Yemen and Saudi Arabia.

Which Gulf country has a high cost of living?

UAE Dubai is costlier than other Gulf countries. In Dubai 90 percent population is expats. Many friends told me that the rent for two BHK apartments in Bahrain is equivalent to one BHK in Dubai. The procedure of getting a Driving license is also very costly in Dubai. Yes, the Standard of living and other facilities are good in Dubai, and it is, in a real sense, a smart city. It has a metro train, buses, taxis, and the world's tallest tower, Burj Khalifa, malls, nightlife, Dubai safari rides and all. In Dubai, UAE, expats are in the majority, and it is a very expat-friendly country. The majority of expats are from India. All major businessmen first came to Dubai, established it, and then expanded to other countries. Many businessmen mainly come from Kerala and live in Dubai. LULU Mall, Kewal Ram, Joyalukkas, Malabar Gold, AL Adil, Nesto, etc., to name a few. Watch their owner's life story on YouTube. It will teach a lot. Similarly many Indians have migrated to African countries like Uganda, Kenya, South Africa etc and became millionaire there.

What care must be taken during sand storm?

Sand storm is regular phenomena in the gulf. Sand moves with air at high velocity and if you walk in open it goes in eyes and ears. Full body dress in the gulf is to prevent body from sand. In morning if you rub eyes it damages eyes as sand get accumulated in the corners. Moving near date tree during windy days also poses risk of damaging eyes as its leaves are very pointed and if pierce in to eye it can damage it. During sand storm car even gets so much sand around it in one day that it looks not cleaned for months.

Chapter

4

Arabic Food

When you go to gulf as an expat, you are going to face the first challenge, which is food. When I reached Yanbu, my company driver took me to a Kerala restaurant as he was from Kerala. Idly dosa is as easily available in gulf as in India due to Kerala people in majority in gulf. For the vegetarian gulf is somewhat difficult as in many places you will not get pure vegetarian restaurants. Many times, it happened that unknowingly vegetarian people eat non-vegetarian food. For non-vegetarian gulf is a paradise. When my son came in the gulf first time I took him to buffet lunch in Arabic restaurant but, he could not eat because it was not spicy.

One day, we had a farewell party for one of our Gujarati friends. We started with soup, of course. At last, some pieces appeared. One friends asked, "What is this? Looks something different" Some replied let us ask Rajenbhai (me) as all knew that I am a global Guajarati and eating occasionally non veg food and drink too. I also said there is something looking like non-veg. Then people went inside and asked cook what it was. The cook said it was chicken sausage pieces. Even though they ordered vegetarian soup, some pieces of chicken came. In Saudi Arabia, we saw small pieces of tuna fish sprinkled on salad.

Another time in Saudi, we were attending one conference. Two Gujarati vegetarian friends were eating mixed vegetables and praising such tasty mix vegetables even they had not tested in India. I was sitting aside with my friend. We were laughing as mutton keema was mixed with mix vegetables. I asked my friend whether to tell them or not. My friend told me Sir why to spoil their mood, what does it make a difference, let them enjoy it. Only halal meat is allowed in the gulf. When Arabic people go abroad, they generally don't eat chicken, meat, and beef because they are not sure if it is halal or not. In the Gulf, pork is prohibited and allowed to non-Muslims only in selected malls.

All leading American food chain brands are available in the gulf like McDonald's, KFC , Subway etc. Coca-Cola tins have taken place as local drinks.

Khabush

Khabush is looking like roti/chapati but it is bread. Available in white and brown colour. Brown is with some fibre, while white is pure fine flour(maida). It is available at a very cheap price. In Saudi, many varieties of khabus are available. In the gulf, without Khabush, no single person can survive, so it is better to get used to it. Khabush is served everywhere in the company canteen restaurant, such as falafel and chicken shawarma. In Bahrain, two main types are available. Plain white and brown khabush.

In Yanbu I saw an automatic khabush plant in one mall and thought that in India also we should start like this type automatic plant. Labourers can eat it and it is also very cheap. We can even sell khabush with potato sabji/bhaji and butter milk and sell khabush bhaji in line with puri bhaji at a very cheap rate. In the gulf without eating khabush you cannot survive.

Falafel

Street food Falafel is vegetable mostly leaves, potato chips and chickpea vada (Tamiya) wrapped in Khabush or chapati. It is a Vegetarian snack and widely used by expats who are vegetarian. Chapati is also used in place of khabush.

Tabbouleh

Tabbouleh is made of fresh parsley, mint, lemon, and bulgur wheat. Parsley is widely used by local people like we Indian use coriander leaves and look wise both looks alike. Some time we make mistake and bring parsley instead of coriander leaves when placed side by side in malls.

Hummus

This is very healthy food, and I like it. Hummus is Arabic chutney prepared by using boiled kabuli big chickpeas, sesame paste(tahini), olive oil, salt and garlic. All crushed together and made a fine paste and decorated with olive oil and green Saur olives. Variation can be obtained by using lemon, bit coriander, green chilly chutney, etc. Local dairies also make hummus. There are many variants available, like plain hummus, lemon hummus, etc. Our Indian mall makes it by fusion with bit and coriander green chilly chutney. I recommend adopting this recipe in India along with coconut chutney, which we get with idly.

Mutabal

Mutabal is similar to the baingan bharta of India, minus the spices. tahini (sesame paste) mixed with grilled brinjal inner pulp, onion, Greek yogurt, salt, garlic and olive oil decorated with pomegranate seed and parsley. This is taken as chutney like hummus with khabush. Many bakeries and restaurants make it and sell it along with other items. I generally take it with grill items as grilled chicken is dry with thin wheat roti.

Khabsa rice

Saudi recipe made from rice using chicken juice. The first chicken piece is cooked using tomato, onion, and other spices. Then a chicken piece is taken out and rice is poured into it and cooked in the cooker. When ready, it is served with a big chicken piece decorated on top of rice. The flavour of chicken is mixed with rice, so it becomes tastier.

Chicken shawarma

This is also street food of gulf and one of my favourite healthy items. The boneless chicken is grilled on a big vertical rod and cut into small pieces using a big knife, mixed with cabbage and potato chips and laban and sesame paste, and wrapped in Khabush or chapati. Whenever I am alone and don't want to cook food, I take two chicken shawarma, and it satisfies my dinner. Also, the chicken and mutton shawarma shop were visible from my room, so it tempted me to eat when I am hungry and tired at East Riffa. Chicken is sold like vegetables and at cheaper rate than vegetables. Frozen chickens are very cheap but hard to digest.

Broasted chicken

Broasted chicken is combination of frying and pressure cooking. Chicken is fried in hot oil with a thick layer of flour on it and then pressure cooked. Sometimes garlic is used to flavour the chicken. In Yanbu I used to visit AL Baik food chain outlet to eat broasted chicken with my friend.

Many brands are very famous in gulf.

Qahwa

Qahwa Arabic coffee with a lot of cardamom. It is taken in a very small cup and finished in one shot. Qahwa is Arabic welcome drinks served on all major festival occasions with dates. More amount of cardamom in Qahwa is a sign of richness. Generally, local people are fond of coffee, cakes, baklawa, chocolates, and grill items. If a local person goes to meet his friend, he will carry Qahwa and cake or chocolates with him.

Dates

When nothing was there in the gulf, the only survival was on dates, camel's meat camel milk and fish. The date is considered pious, and every Arabic house is equipped with dates in gardens like coconut trees and tulsi, which are considered pious plants in India; many types of dates are available in the gulf. In summer, when dates are ripe, half-ripe dates also come into the Gulf market for sale. They have a very fresh taste and are sweet. Both yellow and red dates, later on, get converted to black and light brown in colour when fully ripe. Only drawback is that it has short self-life. Date trees are also coming in male and female so if you plant one tree it may give fruit or not. It should be planted in group. Tree plants planted on road side, and traffic circle looks very beautiful with fruits.

Price is ranging from 1 bd per kg to 20 bd per kg. maj'dul, ajwa, mabroom, safwai, sukari, khodari, khalas, etc. Ajwa date was used by Prophet Mohammed, and it has medicinal value with less sugar. Maj'dul is also a very good date known for its softness and sweetness. Rich people eat dates sandwiched with almonds, walnuts or cashews after the removal of seeds from it. Readymade date packets with sandwiched nuts are available in date and sweet shops. Some Irani dates are also available, which are very soft and economical, but we have to consume them very fast as they deteriorate very fast.

I like majdul, Mabroom and ajwa premium dates. Some make balls using date paste, coconut, and sesame. Also, dates are used as stuffing in biscuits and that is called Maamoul. Date cake also available in the gulf. In old age, dates were piled in one room, and juice coming out of it became a small stream and collected in one small pond. Date syrup prepared this way was used to be exported from Bahrain to other countries. Date wood was used in building materials, and its leaves were used to make huts, so it is kalpavruksh(all parts of the tree are useful) of gulf-like coconut tree in Kerala.

Here in Bahrain and Saudi I saw many dates falling on the ground but nobody eats them. Also, date trees are used as ornament trees on the sides of the road, traffic circles and malls. In Tubli I saw date garden having 700 trees. Dates are miracle tree in the gulf and respected by locals and has impression found on national flags and coins and currency notes. Local employees bring half ripe dates from their date gardens and coffee in office and serve visitors and friends freely.

Biryani

Biryani are mainly made from basmati rice imported from India and Pakistan, nuts, and masala using chicken, mutton, egg, fish, prawns etc. chicken plus rice called chicken biryani, and so on. In restaurants, one BD chicken biryani is available with a lot of rice. People waste rice as they eat half of the dish of biryani and rest throw in the dust bin, it is a major concern during Ramadan. India produces longest Basmati rice.

In one Malayali restaurant I saw jackfruit biryani!

Grills

Many types of grill items are used as food in the gulf. Chicken tikka, mutton tikka, prawn, paneer, onion, etc. mix grills are very famous here in the gulf. Kabab is also available in many versions.

Umm Ali

This is the sweet of the Arabic world. It is simple but tasty. Made from milk, bread and nuts and sugar. One story behind it is such that one king won the war and came back to his home and told his mother good news that he has won. His mother did not have sweets so she made instant sweets by mixing sugar, milk, bread and nuts. Later it became so popular that everywhere in Arabic restaurants you will find this sweet.

Baklava

Baklava is also a sweet item, basically a traditional pastry known for its sweet rich flavour and flaky texture. Tasty and good to carry in India as a novelty sweet. Stuffing is different like nuts, pistachio etc. many good occasions were celebrated by local employee in my company either with chocolates, cake or baklawa.

Sambuusa

Many types of samosa (Arabic name sambuusa) are available in different shape and size. Mainly popular are cheese, chicken, mutton, and vegetable, sweet samosa also available in gulf. Readymade samosa strips also available in malls, you just have to fill the stuffing and fry it. That way a lot of readymade items are available like chicken sausage, chicken nuggets, chicken balls, prawns, mutton and beef items.

Maamoul

This is a biscuit filled with date paste. As in India we stuff coconut in our sweets like Guajarati ghughra similarly Arabic sweets, biscuits and rolls are made using date paste.

Karak tea

This is basically cardamom tea and available at every 10 shops like chicken shawarma. There are many types of tea available in the gulf like saffron tea, ginger tea, mint tea, cardamom tea, hibiscus tea etc. Arabic people like tea without milk which is called sulemani tea.

Generally, with tea Arabic people take local snacks like boiled egg, chickpea, broad beans, dal ful with tameez, dal with khabus sandwiches, cake etc.

Hamour fish

Hamour fish is very popular in the gulf. It has fewer bones and can be made very easily. The fried items are very tasty and cheap. Fish majboosh are made using this fish.

Basa fish

Basa fish is also used in large quantity in gulf as it is bone less and has high quality protein and Omega 3. Basa is banned in India and USA.

Salmon fish

Salmon fish come from cold regions like Alaska USA and Canada of the world and are very costly. It has omega 3 and that is why it is considered very healthy for heart patients. No oil required for cooking as it is full of oil so, just apply salt and pepper and put in a non-stick pan or microwave. Local people cook it with Suva bhaji/Dill leaves to add taste to it as fish has no taste. One of my Filipino friend was eating only salmon and rice and he was claiming he never fall sick.

Dill leaves has medicinal value also for asthmatic patient. In India we cook dill leaves with brinjal potato, tomato, onion and mutter. Just add oil and spices to it and cook in microwave.

When Indian Prime Minister Atal Bihari Bajpai used to visit foreign countries in his lunch menu, the first time I read in the newspaper that salmon fish was on the list, I could taste it in the gulf, as in India, it is not easily available.

Chocolates:

Local people like chocolates and ice creams. There are special chocolate and cheese cake shops. Local people go with friends and family to make party. Branded and local chocolates are available in all major sweet shops and malls. Ice cream also available in all flavour and colors, Yogurt ice cream also consumed widely in gulf.

Cake:

Many good occasions like farewell, birthday and festivals are celebrated in the gulf with cakes. Cheese cake is their favourite item. Cakes are available in various shape and size. Special cake shops are there which are well known for cakes and pastries. Date cakes are variety of gulf. Now all malls also serve cake in their outlets due to increasing craziness of celebrating birth days with cakes.

Harees/Jarees:

Harees is made with cracked wheat and mutton boneless crushed khima. They are boiled in one container with small entry. When harees came to India it is called Haleem which contains cracked wheat, mutton khima, lentil dal, ginger garlic paste and ghee and off course with spices and tadka.

Chapter

5

My Experiences

Why did I change my Indian job?

Many of my friends from the same company had gone to the gulf and settled well, so they were our inspiration to go to gulf. We hear from them that they get 4 times, salary and that is too income tax free. When they arrive in India people see them as an alien and NRI is like status symbol. In Hansot every Muslim family had one person serving in Dubai. Post office was in front of my house. And so many people gather in the morning in front of post office to collect money order sent by relatives from Dubai. Any Muslim youth among them you ask what you will do in future? Only one answer is Dubai jayega, I will go to Dubai. When somebody come from Dubai, he will bring Sony tape recorder, radio, and made in Japan pant and shirt piece.

In India, it was like a dream for us as we were paying 30% of income as income tax, which is almost one-third of our income. Even if NRI send money to India and put in a fixed deposit of NRE account, the interest earned is also tax-free. Many engineers, mainly from the quality control, corrosion and inspection wing, were trying, and they were initially moving in the gulf as QC inspectors and metallurgists. Rotating engineers were also followed in second place. They were hired by multinational companies that manufacture compressors, turbines, and pumps, so they need a country manager and service engineers to maintain their machines worldwide.

In 2002, my company was disinvested by the government of India, and its management was taken over by largest oil and petrochemical giant. After that the situation started changing rapidly, and voluntary retirement started one by one to reduce manpower. The total number of employees were 12,000, and the private company targeted to reduce it to 50 %. They announced a voluntary retirement scheme (VRS). For a 50-plus age employee, it was beneficial; it was like a breakeven point and taking VRS was beneficial, but for people less than 50 years of age, like us, it was not beneficial.

Even when I resigned, my department head told me clearly that I will not be given VRS. If you work hard management will not give VRS, but if you create problems you will get it. One of my friends got it, as management wanted to get rid of him. He got Rs 15 lacs as VRS money. We lost it due to our good work record!!!

Due to the takeover, another major negative change occurred to employees like us. We were given 2 times upgradation, citing that promotion is not possible as vacancies are not there but since we completed resident time in that scale we were upgraded. i.e. UG (upgraded) and SG (second time upgraded) so, we were in the managers pay scale.

During a public sector company, all the benefits were linked to pay scale, so we were getting all the benefits like air LTC, etc., as per pay scale-based manager level entitlement. When the private company took over, all benefits were linked with designation and not the pay scale.

When the new company took over, all smart departments, such as HR, Finance, and Marketing, gave promotions to all their UG and SG employees, except the Operations and Maintenance departments. So, employees in HR, finance, and marketing got promotions, while employees in the operation and maintenance department did not. We felt like we were demoted and started our career once again from ground zero after spending 20 years! Our junior employees in HR, finance and marketing became seniors overnight.

Also, the seniority list was kept aside, and junior-level employees were promoted and made senior, leaving senior employees to choose the "love it or leave it" option. This sentence was often told by my ex-boss that you have 2 options. You love it or leave it. In other words, you accept that your junior officer will be your boss or resign from the post and leave the company and be happy. The SAP merit rating system was introduced. Bonus and increments were based on the rating given to you by your top boss. There were 4 categories. Poor, Good, very good, and excellent. Poor will not get anything and may get fired, good will get something, very good will get more and excellent will get the highest; in other words, a good rating was not at all good money-wise.

In this situation, I started searching for a job change very sincerely, as I wanted to come out from this humiliation, frustration and demotion. I appeared for many interviews in Bombay, but they were negative. My majority Saturdays and Sundays were spent travelling from Baroda to Bombay by Baroda Express and coming back by Sunday night by the same train. It was very convenient to travel by Baroda Express as all night journeys pass by sleeping on the train, finishing work on time, and no hotel stay no leave required.

Suddenly, one day, I saw an advertisement in the newspaper regarding mechanical engineers for KSA. The interview was at the newly opened Baroda branch office of a Bombay manpower agent, who was mainly hiring for Gulf oil and gas companies. I went for an interview after taking a half-day leave from my company, and based on my experience and interview, they selected me for the post of Mechanical project engineer. After some days, I got an appointment letter from a Saudi manpower supply company owned by one of the princes of Saudi Arabia. At that time, we did not have internet and printers at home, so I used to visit a nearby cybercafé for internet and emails. I got my first Gulf job offer letter printed and felt very happy. The cafe owner also asked me congratulations how you got this job?

Now, after the offer letter, it was the responsibility of the manpower agent company to lend me safely to Saudi Arabia. So now my case was handled by a separate visa officer. She was a lady HR officer. After some days, I had to go to Bombay for a medical test, which I completed. Then they asked me to go to New Delhi for a degree certificate attestation and stamping from the Ministry of Human Resource department and the Ministry of External Affairs of the Government of India. Stamping on a degree certificate from the Saudi embassy is also required. I took 5 days' leave from the office, taking New Delhi Agra LTC. The company gave every two years travel reimbursement to the family to visit tourist places. Earlier, all these attestation formalities were completed by the agent office located in New Delhi, but as there were some instances of fake documents, the government made it compulsory for candidates to appear personally for all attestation.

We were staying at my company guest house in a posh locality of New Delhi, where I met some other friends who came there to stamp on degree certificates. They also did not disclose openly except for one. First, we went to the ministry of HRD. There was a long queue at morning 5 am. The situation was so grim that job aspirants had to stand outside, and all agents were roaming nearby in big numbers. They offer to finish the work for 500 Rs. But my friends made me aware that I should not go through agents as they sometimes cheat candidates and disappear with original certificates. In the morning, the government office collects applications with certificates, and in the afternoon, they give them back duly signed and stamped.

Then we went to the Ministry of External Affairs for stamping, but the time was over, so we had to go the next day. I planned 5 days that was comfortable considering 3 days' work and 2 days extra. Other friends came with 2 to 3 days' leave and faced problems as matters could not be completed. On the second day, we went to the Ministry of External Affairs. There were 2 lines, one for graduates and one for non-graduates. Later, they announced that they would make one line only. That created chaos among candidates as candidates started fighting, and some also tore off certificates. Police came to the rescue and solved it somehow. In the afternoon, we got our certificates stamped.

On the 3rd day, we went to the Saudi embassy to submit an engineering degree certificate for stamping. There were also 2 lines, one for agents and a second for applicants. The line of applicants was very long, and it seems we may not get a turn. But my wife was with me, and she observed that some ladies were coming out very fast, and there was a separate line for ladies. She took an application form and a degree certificate from me and submitted it within no time. This helped me to complete the procedure fast. My friend was in line, but he took a long time. Later, he came to request me that I collect his certificate from the Saudi embassy as he had to return to Baroda by night train. After collecting certificates from the embassy, we went to the agent's office in New Delhi to submit my passport, CV and certificates. He had to finish the rest of the visa stamping at the embassy. After 10 days, he sent me a passport with a visa stamp. Now he has advised me to resign as within 3 months, I have to reach Yanbu in the western part of Saudi Arabia on the Red Sea side to join a petrochemical company.

Side by side, I started contacting friends in Saudi Arabia who work in different locations. The only benefit of working in a big refinery or petrochemical company in the oil and gas sector in India is that we already have some friends working at all major oil and gas companies in the Gulf. We can contact them through friends and networks, and they will guide us properly because when they went there, they used the same technique to get the knowledge and information, so they were happy to share it with their ex-company engineer. Indeed, it was to feel like giving back to society. My batchmate friend sent me the email address of his friend who was working in the same manpower supply company at Yanbu to which I was going. He encouraged me like anything, and I still remember his words: come and see the outside world.

My Indian company was passing through many changes every day. One day we found out that the notice period of resignation was changed from 1 month to 3 months to discourage young engineers from resigning. I had to join there as early as possible, so I requested my new employer company about this new law, and they said they would pay me a one-month salary if I gave documentary evidence of payment of money through receipt. I decided to serve for one and a half months and pay for one and a half months. I encashed my leave first before my resignation and then kept money ready to pay the balance of my home and car loan and notice period. This sequence was very much required because if I resign and ask for leave encashment, the company will not settle it as I have already resigned, and they will lock my salary and ask me to pay all pending loans before settlement. Many friends had to take out loans to pay for company loans because they had resigned first and then applied for leave encashment.

Now, as per schedule, I resigned and sent the papers to my immediate boss. He signed and sent it to his higher-ups. The section head was very surprised and scared, also. First of all, he couldn't believe that I was resigning. He said I am not going to give you a VRS (voluntary retirement scheme). In those days, employees above 50 years were taking VRS and management induced new blood, willingly relieving them. I said I don't want any VRS, so just approve my resignation that is sufficient for me. Then he said, I will approve your resignation and get the signature of higher management; you need not go to them. I said I was not interested at all in meeting anybody. My senior boss went to HOD for his approval, but the heads of the department insisted on meeting with me. So now he was forced to tell me to meet the head of department HOD. He said the boss wanted to meet me. I said ok, if he wants, I will meet.

The next day morning, I met him. He started very casually asking where I was going. I replied frankly that I was going to petrochemical company at Yanbu, Saudi Arabia. He asked whether it was the eastern side or the western side. I said the western side. He said don't go there as on the western side there was a terrorist attack and shooting and the terrorists killed some western expats. One eyewitness narrated this incident. He said that the area is not safe. I replied, "Sir, I have made up my mind to quit and now don't want to change it". He said even though you have decided, today you go home and think twice discuss with family and come tomorrow morning if you want to go, collect a file from my office. I will sign it. The next day, I collected a file from his office. He was a nice person, and he made his comments in a positive manner.

After submitting a resignation approved file to HR for further process, again a new problem came. Now the site in charge wanted us to take money paid in lieu of notice period back and serve for the whole 3 months' notice period. This was a totally impractical demand. As visa issued are for 3 months only and if we resign after getting visa in hand it will be less than 3 months.

Actually, in 2006, 25 engineers resigned together en masse, and the site in charge was worried how much impact will come on company. He thought if he asked for money to be paid without encashing leaves, the engineer would not go. But engineers started repayment by arranging money from other sources. The HR in charge came to meet me personally; he told me frankly that we could not ask such unethical demands from you as you served the company for so many years sincerely, but as the site in charge insists, they cannot do anything but obey. He suggested that I meet the site in charge personally and try to convince him. I asked for an appointment from his PA and went to meet him. I tried to convince him, but he insisted on serving for 3 months and said we would pay you a salary for it as if he was doing me a great favour! I was very angry but could not talk much. I was going to tell him that I am not a bonded labour and that he should respect my dignity. But I controlled my temper. After coming out, I decided to take some legal action. I met another friend, M, who also resigned and wanted to go to the KSA for a job. He was also of the same opinion about going legal.

We met an ex-HR manager who started practising as a lawyer in court after retirement from my company. He asked for our original appointment order and said you will be governed by the terms and conditions of your appointment letter and the notice period mentioned in it. It was 1 month, as mentioned in my appointment letter. He said I will give you one para-legal letter; you just post it before going along with a copy of your appointment letter, payment receipt; management cannot do anything to your balance money payment like PF, salary, etc. We both did the same and, after going, just asked the family to post the letter by registered post to office of site in charge. After 1 month, I found that management released all of us without any action. The site in charge might have referred the letter to the legal section, and the legal section must have advised him that if employees go to court, employees will win, which would create a bad impression of the company in the country.

When I resigned and went to the salary section, they praised me, saying that with proper planning, I paid all the dues and loans, and some employees went without paying due money and loans. I told the salary section officer that if I paid all my dues now, you don't have any right to withhold my settlement payment. Even the CEO of the company and I are now equal in the eyes of the law as we both are citizens of India. He agreed and said he did not even agree with his boss' suggestion to hold the payment. He argued with his boss that if an employee goes to court, who will protect him?

In my department, some friends were not ready to believe that I would resign. One day, another friend and I, who suffered in same manner as me due to privatisation of company. We were of the opinion that now this is the high time to leave the company. My nearby seating colleague M just jumped off the seat and said, 'I challenge you both, that none of you will leave and if any one of you is going, I will give you a golden ring from my side as a gift". I could not stop laughing. I said to H that some well-wishers are more confident than us that we will not leave the company. When I told friend M that today I paid my home loan by giving an INR 5 lacs check to the HR loan section, he whispered slowly, now it looks like you are going.

I used to give farewell addresses and anchoring facilities whenever there was any retirement party in my department. I even wrote an essay, "VRS Mitro ne", for friends who opted for the Voluntary Retirement Scheme and distributed copies to all who had taken VRS. It was about what to do after retirement. One day, a friend called me; he said, you have written a very good essay, and daily I read it. It feels good. This article and another article on Raag therapy was published in the local Guajarati magazine Feelings. My department friends wanted to give me farewell, but I refused as I did not want to create any impression that I was going early. I wanted to give surprise.

I also started packing my bags as the departure date was coming close and, in my company, I told them one week after the departure date so that no surprise would come now. I was to go one day in advance and stay in Mumbai with one of our relatives as the Saudi flight was the next day morning. I went to Mumbai and stayed at Borivali at a relative's house. They booked a car for me, so I went in early in the morning. At the airport, agents' men came to give me a file with all my passport, visa and relevant documents and stayed there to see my boarding pass to confirm that I was going. Payments to agents are made only when employees reach and report at the client company. That is why agents make sure that selected candidate board the plane. Sometime some expat has two to three offers in hand and join one company who give maximum salary, some candidate after accepting offer negotiate in their Indian company and get promotion and do not join the gulf job. For that now gulf company blacklist those candidates.

At the airport, Saudi Airlines asked all passengers to hand over their bags and cargo. My important papers, like the joining document file which was given by agent, were also handed over to the counter as cargo baggage. At the immigration counter, the immigration officer asked me to show the offer letter from the Saudi company. I wanted to prove that I was going for employment purposes. He said nowadays, terrorist activity has increased, and we have to ask for all supporting documents from Gulf immigrants. I replied that I had handed over all my handbags as cargo and I was going for the first time, so it was my mistake. I am sorry about that, and next time, it will be taken care of. He said if you were at another counter, you would be in trouble, but I will let you go. I thanked him, and finally, he stamped my exit stamp, and I went for departure. Now I am out of India. Saudi Airlines planes are very large as the same planes are used for hajj pilgrims; @2.5 million pilgrims go for hajj from worldwide every year. Our flight left at 10 am for Saudi Arabia. The majority were expatriates like me who were going for employment purposes.

The plane of Saudi airline was very big and spacious. They call it a hajj plane, which is very large in size. Haj is the second largest business of Saudi Arabia after oil. Before take-off there was a prayer broadcast on the screen as per Islamic tradition. After take-off the air hostess started distributing lunch. It was biryani and there were only two options, chicken biryani and lamb biryani. So, she was simply asking chicken, lamb, chicken, lamb...

Yanbu experience

My flight was from Mumbai to Jeddah via Riyadh. We reached Riyadh the capital of KSA, where we had to clear immigration as from Riyadh to Jeddah, it was a local domestic flight. At Riyadh, immigration stamping on passports was done, and a vaccine was given. From Riyadh to Jeddah, it was a 2-hour journey. At Jeddah airport, I met Mr. Patel, who was a civil engineer serving in a cement company through the same manpower supply company that I was joining at Yanbu. He gave me initial information about Yanbu and our contracting company. I was feeling relieved as I got some guidance now, and that is the same company. In other countries, if you find somebody from your own country, you feel comfortable having to spend 4 hrs at Jeddah airport as the Yanbu flight was in the evening. At Jeddah, there was some rain, so we felt a cool atmosphere.

In the evening, we reached Yanbu, and our company driver came to receive me with my name on the display board in hand. Patel also came with me as he knew the driver. The driver dropped me in my room and gave me the key to the door. There were about 10 rooms. The common kitchen had all the basic amenities like a fridge, gas stove, kitchenware, and utensils. All new employees come there and land in a company guest house till he makes his own arrangements for the rental house. Initially, it was also convenient as many formalities like iqama (country ID card), bank account opening, and identity badge from client company were to be completed. All required papers are to be submitted to HR men who were working as an office in charge and the Yanbu office head who was working as a (BDM) business development manager. There were 4 drivers (2 Indian and

2 Saudi) and one local Saudi govt relation officer also, so a total 7 staff in the company office and about 200 engineers and technical staff were working in various company like petrochemicals and refineries, etc. On 31 January 2007, I reported to HR men, and he asked me whether I was ready to go for a job; I replied yes, and he asked the Saudi officer to take me and drop me at the petrochemical company. HR men and driver were from Kerala, and P was very cooperative. He was working as a single window point of contact for all employee requirements like all claims, Iqama, family visa, family ticket, vacation, medical reimbursement, etc.

One Saudi officer came with me to drop by car at the company premises. We started our journey for a petrochemical company. From the remote, I saw the chimney of heaters of an olefins plant, and he asked me if it was a petrochemical co. I said yes. He was happy that I could identify the company. At the entrance, one office assistant came to receive me at the gate. He arranged my visitor pass and took me with him. I met superintendent of Core maintenance, Reliability. he expressed surprise at my coming as my hiring talk was on hold in between. I asked for a higher salary, and he said he did not know further progress after that. He welcomed me and asked me to meet the supervisor of fixed/stationery equipment. He informed me that I would be working as a focal point for inventory management. I will have to handle vendor spec queries for stock item. He showed me my cabin and also arranged a new table, chair, and phone nos. He informed me that he would arrange a desktop computer for me within a short time. Every day I read some articles from documents about the company, as the document department was very near the same floor. There were 8 engineers in my section.3 Indians, 3 Saudi, 1 Pakistani and 1 Filipino. I was attached to one Indian engineer who was from Chennai for orientation.

I was assigned to resolve fixed equipment-related queries coming from suppliers and vendors. This job was generated due to SAP material management software. For inventory stock items, the SAP material management system automatically generates an RFQ (request for quotation) when the quantity falls below the minimum order level, and enquiry goes to suppliers; as it is a system-generated RFQ, the materials department requires one focal point to whom they can send a vendor query. For non-stock items, this was not required since engineers who raise purchase requisition (PR) have to answer those queries. Another main reason for the query was that every engineer was empowered to create material numbers in SAP, and nobody checked whether complete specifications were mentioned or not. In some materials, like gaskets or heat exchangers, vendors ask for drawings; in some cases, the material is not specified properly, dimensional standards are not mentioned, the material grade is not specified, etc. The query kept on coming as there were many materials as stock items for pipes, fittings, flanges, valves, bolt nuts, gaskets, heat exchangers, tube bundles, tubes, gaskets, tube plugs, heat exchanger gaskets, structural steel, workshop consumable material, crane material, etc. About more than 10,000 stock numbers were there.

In the evening, I met business development manager BDM and complained that I had been given the title of project engineer and assigned to the maintenance department. I had experience in the project department, whereas I was deputed in the maintenance department. I asked how I would work as I don't have experience in maintenance. He advised me to work for 3 months as he would arrange for another engineer as a replacement, and only then could he transfer me. He also advised that in India, he was selling lubrication oil, and here in Saudi, he was selling manpower. So, it is good to take change as a challenge and take all types of different experiences. After that, I talked to my colleagues and engineers who were working in the project department about this, and I saw that they were all eager to move to my place and come to the maintenance department!!

Later I came to know that working in maintenance brings us close to company top management and there is ample chance to get direct employment in place of a contract employee. There were two types of employment in gulf through contracting companies like us and we were called contract employees and, on the company, hired were called direct hire employees.

In a project it becomes like an employee of contractor's contractor. Contract companies deploy manpower and project companies get purchase orders from main companies for particular project. So, after the project is over, they are shifted from one company to another. While in maintenance department it is like a permanent job with one company and one boss only. In the project each project engineer has to cater to so many sister companies at a time.

Then, I also found that my new job was not that different. It was the same but having different areas like dealing with materials query. Specification Query was like puzzles, some time it takes minutes and some time hours and sometime days also. For example if I want to procure pipe I have to mention whether it is seamless or welded, diameter, thickness or schedule number, material specification as per ASME(earlier ASTM) dimensional standard as per ASME etc. if any one item missed it will come as spec query from vendor who received this RFQ.

In the evening, the driver took me to a Kerala restaurant, and I took an idly sambhar. Idly (also called rice cake) and dosa are basically south Indian dishes but have now become famous throughout India and are now internationally considered as the top 26 breakfasts in the world. It is light as steamed food, and the sambhar (dal with vegetables like brinjal, tomato, moringa sticks, potato, pumpkin etc. soup) and coconut chutney are very tasty and cheap, so it has become worldwide recipe in line with pizza.

Due to change of food I got stomach infection, I became sick, so I went to the doctor at the nearby Al Shifa hospital. There was one Indian doctor who gave me 500 mg. tablet. The initial culture shock and homesickness were also there feeling like detached from country, culture and family.

In Saudi Arabia, there are Pakistani and Indian Malayali restaurants available. In Yanbu, one Pakistani paratha centre was very famous, where aloo paratha, methi paratha, and muli paratha were served with Chana sabji at a very reasonable rate of 1 Saudi Riyal. Sometimes, we used to take food at both places to make a change. Arabic restaurant also we were frequently visiting. Arabic food has very few spices and is mainly dry, like biryanis, khabsa rice, broasted chicken, mutton tikka, chicken tikka and kebabs. Chicken shawarma and falafel are also very popular items.

Initially, I stayed for 1 month in a guest house, and then our company Hyderabadi driver, K, arranged a house for us three Indians who had recently joined the same company. I was from Gujarat, S is from Bihar, and V is from Tamil Nadu like mini India. We were in a bachelor house with a common kitchen and drawing room. The flat was on the ground floor. In Saudi Arabia, bachelors have to stay in bachelor's houses. They cannot stay in a family apartment. In one building, bachelor and married families cannot stay together even in separate flats. Rules were very strict, and religious police called mutawa were very frequently visiting the bachelor homes. They conduct checks, and if found violating the laws, the next day, he may be in jail or out of the country. We purchased initial items like a cot, mattress, bucket, tumbler stand for drying clothes, a/c machine, etc. V was Tamil, so he spoke little with us in English as he did not know Hindi. Sometimes, S was taunting him; "you are Indian and do not know Hindi?" With S, we had a good time as I was cooking veg and he was cooking non-veg dishes for us. We were taking it with Khabush chapati, like Arabic bread, which was available in many varieties made of Maida, wheat flour, etc. There was an automatic khabush bakery in Yanbu Mall to manufacture these Khabush. Khabush was travelling on a metallic chain conveyor, passing through the oven and coming out at the end, and it would fall and make a big heap of Khabush. Khabus are very helpful to bachelors as roti making is a skilled job. S had a car, so it was very useful for getting food and water bottles.

In Saudi, all families have cars, and you cannot find bicycles, rickshaws or scooters like in India. Also, due to the very hot and humid weather, you cannot walk easily in the open sun light. A car with AC is a must. After coming back to Saudi Arabia, he purchased a car. 20-litre water bottles sold at all cold stores were used for drinking water. Generally, we keep 2 to 3 bottles so that it can last for one month. Whenever it is empty, we go by car and get it filled by the nearby RO water plant. Room was completely dark. Windows were covered with stickers and closed forever, so to confirm whether it was day or night, we had to go outside of the house. The House owner was an 80-year-old Saudi man. He was always seated outside near entrance in the evening. If anybody did not pay rent, he would be stopped from entering the house. One caretaker, a Bangladeshi boy, was taking care of him. He was taking him to hookah or shisha bars. As per his caretaker, the house owner was still interested in marrying at the age of 80 years! Many old people from gulf visits Hyderabad for marriage.

During the day we have lunch in the company canteen. Morning 6 am to evening 6 pm was our duty time as we had to compensate for an additional 2 hrs daily for holiday on Thursday. Every day, I have to wake up at 4 am to catch the company minibus at 5 am and reach the duty point at 6 am. For company direct hire employees, working hours were 40 hours whereas, for contract employees like me, it was 48 hours per week, so, daily, we have to overstay for 2 hours for 4 days. Many contract employees were working with us, so it was not a problem to pass the time. One Filipino engineer from the same company was also there, so generally, we discussed common things. He was a very intelligent and soft-spoken person and religious too. One day he told me you cannot go to heaven without Jesus!

Our company provided transport for all employees in minibus vans. Saudi drivers were driving the van very fast. One driver, K, was so fast that we generally used to say close your eyes and sit; you will reach the destination, either home or heaven! One day, he was driving so slowly. I asked K why he was driving so slowly. He showed me one place where a van was burnt along with the driver after a head-on collision with a date tree on the road. All industries were nearby, so they would drop one by one and collect similarly in the evening. If some do not want to avail company transport, he has to arrange his own car or come in friend's car and give monthly lumpsum money to friend. In Saudi, second-hand used cars were very cheap, and petrol was cheaper than water (40 halal (paisa) per litre, whereas water was 1 riyal per litre). So many employees who bring families have to purchase a car as public transport was not available that easily. Generally, for 1 to 2 years all travel by company transport as contract employees change jobs faster than direct hire company employees. Car selling gives an indication that he is leaving, so nobody purchases a car who wants to change jobs in short time.

The value and advantage of direct hire were more as they

had a 5-day week,40 working hours and a company bonus they were getting, which was equivalent to 2 to 4 times the monthly basic salary. I was employed by a contract company in the reliability department of the fixed equipment group. I was working as a spec query engineer in a fixed equipment group. Generally, 100 material-related queries were received daily from procurement by our department focal point A. He was then forwarding me. After some months, he was also removed from the line, so I was getting it directly from the procurement department focal point, who was Z from Pakistan. In Saudi Arabia, all third-world countries expatriates work mainly from India, Pakistan, and the Philippines. Indians are a respected community among them and are mainly doing upper-level jobs like engineering, operations, and maintenance, project business jobs. Pakistanis mainly work in the transport and hotel business. Bangladeshis work in janitorial service and car cleaning. Nepalis mainly work in hotels and non-technical jobs like security and scaffolding workers. The Philippines are mainly in-house maid jobs and some in hotel industries; a few were with us also as designer and engineer jobs.

In the gulf, Governments have fixed quotas for each country so that one country does not become a monopoly. Also, there are different salary structures for different nationalities. The Asian countries are India, Pakistan, Bangladesh, and Nepal. American salary covers America and the American continent, European countries, and Middle Eastern Arabic countries. Americans are getting the maximum salary. Some Pakistani and Indian engineers go to the UK, USA, or Canada. Study there and then come to the Middle East with an American, British, or Canadian passport to get an American salary. Local people's salaries were in between. Surprisingly, though they are equal or less intelligent, Singapore and Malaysian engineers are getting European salaries. One of my friends was a GM in a labour supply company in Saudi Arabia. He used to say that they recruit people from Nepal and give one month of training in a workshop to tighten and open bolts and nuts, fix gaskets, etc. When they go to work, the client complains that workers don't know anything! Due to visa quota limits for different countries, they cannot bring technically skilled labour from India, where they are available.

In Arabic culture, if you don't know the name of any person, you can call him Mohammed like a brother dada or uncle in India. Mohammed is the world's largest name. The driver, electrician, and car mechanic are all named Mohammed, so we have to save phone numbers as electrician Mohammed or driver Mohammed, etc. It is better to say salaam walekum (hello) instead of good morning. You may experience some local people not saying good morning in response. Drivers and police generally don't understand English, so we have to learn some words and numbers in Arabic, which is not the case in Bahrain. In Bahrain many Bahraini speaking Hindi easily. Best way to learn Arabic numbers is watching car numbers on number plate of Saudi cars because they write in English and Arabic.

In Saudi Arabia, if you are Muslim and not praying, religious police (mutawa) will catch you and leave you in a remote place in the desert, so you have to come by walking. One day, my friend was sitting on the bank steps, and he was caught by Mutawa, seeing his unsaved face. He said, "Mafi Muslim", which means I am not Muslim, and then he was relieved; at the time of prayer, all Mutawas would come in the pick-up car and take a round of the city. And ask all to go for prayer saying salah salah. In a shop or mall also, if it is prayer time, you have to wait till it opens after prayer. The shop owner will ask you to wait for 5 minutes till they come back from prayer.

S, my flat partner's bed was like a small industrial engineers' workbench. Everything was within reach of 1-meter radius. One mattress was in the centre of the room at the ground, and all required things were in a radius of 1 meter. Mobile, Clothes, tea mug, cigarettes and shoes. He was drinking tea in the same cup in which he used to put cigarette buds. I asked him why he smokes so much. His answer was that he could not drink. I asked, "Why are you not drinking?" He said it is haram. I said, "See, I am not drinking or smoking." He had no answer. I said you can quit smoking if you want.

It will improve your health. Anyway, I enjoyed his company as he was very humble and well mannered. He respected me due to my elder age. Friday Saturday I was feeling lonely as S was travelling every week either Makkah or Madinah by his car.

As our room was on the ground floor, there was a great problem with rats. During the night, rats used to visit all the rooms and cut things. They come out from bathrooms European toilets. V was harassed like anything by rats. His AC machine wire was cut, and many things were damaged by rats. One day, he brought sticking pads on which a rat was to stick, but unfortunately, his leg was stuck on it! The next day, he saw one rat, and he took a stick, ran behind it and killed it with a stick.

I moved to new place after some time as S was also moving in family house as his wife was coming from India. One of the operators of the new project company had started a guest house for bachelors. N1 started room on rent in a bachelor house. He took 6 BHK house at 15000 Saudi riyals per year, furnished some minimum furniture like beds, cupboards, etc, and started giving it to us on a per-room basis. We were paying 200 riyal per month so we 5 were paying him 1000 riyal per month. We were also comfortable as the kitchen was common, and cooking was fun as everyone collectively took on different tasks like vegetable cutting, cooking, utensil cleaning, etc. I was handling accounts.

Myself, G, S, A, M and F were the room holders in the same apartment. N1 was ruling like a leader. He was following the vegetarian food. He said I have a condition with arbab houseowner, and if you take non-vegetarian food in the room, he will kick you out. I thought he was bluffing with us as the local house owner himself was eating non-veg. How will he stop others from eating? But we were keeping silent as it was fun when you lived together in a bachelor's house. If you are alone, it is difficult to cook every day, and it makes it difficult to pass the time during holidays. Here work was divided and each member will share his company experiences so time was passing very fast with fun. N1 came from a Singapore based American multinational oil company, so he told many stories about Singapore, saying that it is very expensive and you cannot save more. He said, "In Singapore, you can choose fish from a fish tank, and the cook will fork it out and directly fry it in a hot oil pan without cleaning and serve you."

N2 was from a private petrochemical company in India, and he came there as a training manager. On Friday and Saturday, we generally have bachelors made dinner or lunch parties and then walk at the Red Sea shore near the fish market. The atmosphere of Yanbu was very pleasant, and humidity was not a big problem there. It was on the opposite end of Egypt on the Red Sea. He was telling us the history of his Hazira based ex company and how it was made from ex-employees of other government oil and petrochemicals and fertilizers and other industries. N2 was not from any group so he was feeling lonely. He changed many companies in very little time. His many friends settled in America and Canada. One Mr. S came to the higher post as vice president in new company in Yanbu. He brought many people to his team from an Indian company, and N2 was one of those teams.

G was a sleeping man. On holidays, he will sleep only. He will awake for lunch, and then he will sleep again. In the morning, if we wake him up for tea and breakfast, he will be angry about why his sleep was spoiled. He was working in the procurement department as a buyer. When his boss got transferred to Al Jubail, he also came with him. He was a very nice person. We generally go to Dammam to shop in my car with his wife and son when my family visits Saudi. He is now settled in Australia with his family, and he is an Australian citizen with two kids.

A was from my ex-company, and he had joined a new company. He was a very typical Punjabi guy. His Punjabi lifestyle was very interesting. Every 2 or 3 hrs, he will ask to make some food, let us eat fruit, and let us drink milk at night. He liked cooking and drive others out of kitchen "You people go out; I will cook." He was very crazy. On the other end, N was in the mode of saving money. He said that A is consuming our money like anything; you take control of money, he asked me. Earlier, when he was not present, N1 and his friend did not allow us to cook. Only the vegetable-cutting job was coming to us. But when A came, they were also thrown outside. We were very happy. He used to cook very fast. chapati he was making with chanting prayer Hanuman Chalisa. One day instead of milk, he poured buttermilk because both were coming in the same size container, and the price and thickness were also the same. Even I made a mistake and once brought milk instead of buttermilk. Everyone started eating with hotchpotch (rice and mung dal mix recipe) and milk. Suddenly, N1 identified and asked what I had brought. I said buttermilk. He said no, you made a mistake. You brought milk. I said what difference does it make? It will become buttermilk once it enters the stomach! Buttermilk is called Laban in the gulf.

N1 was a very clever guy. He used to wear a Singapore-based American company jacket to show that he came from a multinational American company in Singapore. He will send all his money to India prior to vacation and borrow money from us for shopping and he will tell me I have to take laptop for my son and daughter as they asked for it. Please give me some money. So, we gave him. He will return after coming back from vacation. He was suffering from diabetes and high blood pressure. He used to measure sugar from blood. He brought one machine for measuring blood sugar. When it did not show proper reading, he threw it on the ground with one bad word. I asked him why he threw the machine. What is the fun in breaking it?

He used to bring a lot of snacks from India, about 20kg. Daily, he would open one packet and give us some for tasting. He used to call me into his room and ask me to sing some old Hindi movie songs. I had done a 6-year course, Sangeet Visharad BA with vocal music and 1-year Sugam sangeet, which helped me to establish as singer wherever I go. Classical music teaches about taal and sur whereas Sugam teaches how to express words with its meaning. Mean "dur" should be sung as "duuuur," showing the real distance between words. My knowledge of singing gave me good attraction from friends, and many times we had some singing parties. We went to Jeddah for a bachelor tour. We hired a taxi and went to a very beautiful mall. In the mall, it was like natural scenery with a lot of plants and waterfalls.

Cats in Saudi Arabia are like tigers, as dogs are not there, and they get ample food, such as chicken and mutton bones, from dust beans. They become very big in volume. If you throw trash bags in dust beans, 3 to 4 cats will jump out from it. In Saudi, you cannot throw Khabush (bread like roti) in dustbins. It has to be hanged. If some local person sees it, he will scold you. Still food wastage is a big problem in the gulf. A big biryani plate they will order and half of it they throw in dustbins. Also, steel scrap is not collected from roads, so you find many hangers, wires, kills and Coca-Cola tins on the street. So, I felt if magnets with roller cars are regularly tripped, many nails and metallic scrap will stick on, and in that way, many cars can be saved from puncture also.

Daily morning in office after morning meeting we gather in pantry room for tea and coffee which was free from company. Pakistani friend in my department was mixed with us and speaking same Hindi language. But Tamil friend was odd men out, he was not able to speak Hindi. Whenever we talk Hindi, he will say English English. When we speak English, our Saudi friend will ask, you are Indian why you speak English? I had to explain them that India is very big country and we have more than 1000 languages. He doesn't know Hindi and I don't know his language Tamil so common language English we are talking.

One day Pakistani friend called us for lunch at his house. he served us biryani, kabab and Zamzam water after meal which he brought from Makkah. One day I told him you got mixed up with us so nicely that you look Indian only. He confessed his forefathers migrated from Bihar to Pakistan during partition in 1947. In the gulf many Indian and Pakistani family live peacefully and unitedly in one building and help each other like same countrymen. One local friend told me his Pakistani worker brought one Sikh to work with him, I told him because their mother tongue is same Punjabi.

AL Jubail experience

I was selected for petrochemicals company at Al Jubail as a direct hire employee my dream job.

I got appointment order so I resigned and went back to India. I landed in Bombay on 3 September during Ramadan 2008 from Yanbu. I thought that I would be able to complete the visa formality and be able to join in October 2009, but as Ramadan is the month of fasting, working hours and speed are greatly reduced in this month. Also, during Ramadan, due to the rush of the Hajj pilgrimage, there was a piling of 10000 passports for Saudi visas, so I had to stay one more month, and I could only join in November 2008 at Al Jubail.

I was to travel before Diwali as the ticket was booked by an agent just one week before Diwali, so I requested to postpone it by one week, but they declined. I wanted to enjoy Diwali with my family at Vadodara when I went to the airport the agent's call came, so I contacted them again. The agent said I had to postpone my journey and advised me to take a rest and enjoy Diwali with my family. I went back with the family, who came to drop me off at Vadodara airport. Later on, I came to know that they didn't have hotel accommodation for me at Al Jubail, so the company asked the agent to postpone my joining.

After Diwali, my ticket was booked for 4 November; I landed at Dammam airport, one Pakistani driver came to pick me up from the Dammam airport. He asked me where I had to go at Al Jubail. I replied I don't know. He said his boss told him that I knew the place. I said my friends were given accommodation in an Intercontinental hotel. He said he would drop me off at Intercontinental and go. I said no, you ask your boss. I am coming to Al Jubail for the first time and don't know anything. Then he called his boss and got the correct destination. It was Hotel K in Fanateer area.

They allocated me 2 BHK fully furnished apartments with an 800-litre fridge but no food inside. The hotel was charging 750 SR per day for this flat from the company. The hotel was new, so no dining facility was opened. I went to the reception and asked where to go for food. They gave me one mobile number and asked me to order. I contacted them and tried what was on the menu. He told me about many items but could not understand, but biryani was a repeated word, so I ordered chicken biryani. After some time, one person came with a packet in hand. I gave him ten-riyal and took a packet.

Next day I went to complete joining formalities at company headquarters which was at a walkable distance from the hotel. They gave me one contract paper for signature. One side was in English and the other side was in Arabic on the same page. Signed on each page and returned back to complete further signature from company president. Next two days were holidays being Friday and Saturday weekends.

So, the HR representative asked me to rest at the hotel and asked me if I could join the company on Sunday.

In the gulf there are five types of salary structure for each region of the world. North American was the highest and eastern was the lowest salary.

1.   Saudi Salary

2.   North American salary

3.   European salary

4.   Mid-eastern salary

5.   Eastern salary

It was difficult to pass 2 days as no known face was seen in the Fanateer area. It was a royal area and was known as the Royal Commission area. On the seashore is a developed walking track called Cornish, so in the evening, many Saudi ladies and gents come for a walk.

I went to Jubail City by taxi, where my friend U was staying. He joined the same company and the same department that I was supposed to join. He was from my ex-company in India, he was from another complex, and I was from the Vadodara. I went Delhi for the first time for my document stamping from the Saudi Embassy and the Ministry of HR and External Affairs Government of India. He was going to join Rabigh, and I was going for Yanbu. he also met me during an interview at Hotel Taj in Mumbai. I kept email contact with him and asked him to book for me also in the bachelor's first apartment.

In Al Jubail, this was a good arrangement provided by the owner of the first apartment, a fully furnished apartment with all basic amenities like a sofa bed, TV, kitchen utensils, fridge, dining table etc. 3 people could stay together in one apartment, and the rent was 3000 Riyal per month, so 1000 Riyal per head, it was quite comfortable. I was staying with U and another friend who came from fertilizer company Bharuch India; he was working in a private company in Al Jubail. In his fertilizer company, there was a very good facility for employees. The company was giving one-year leave without pay, so if an employee wants to go and join a Gulf company, he can go work and come back within 1 year if found not suitable, so it is like a voluntary retirement scheme VRS.

The next day, I went to the company by a minibus with my friend from the bus stop near my building. He had lined up all the joining requirements for me, so the clerk came to pick me up from the gate, and the security made a temporary gate pass for me. I met my department manager, who was American and working from the American company side within my new company, which had a joint venture with a local company. In Saudi Arabia, many joint venture companies have American Saudi companies 50:50 JV. I also met my Arabic boss, who carried out my interview in

India. I was welcomed by them, my American Boss told me that he was waiting for me.

The project department was set up 2 years before to cater for small brownfield projects worth 10 million SAR; above 10 million were considered major projects which were assigned to other sister concern project companies. Initially, it took 3 months to get settled in Al Jubail. The company ID, Iqama, bank account, etc. took one month. Then, I started for a family visa and driving license.

The first day started with a medical test at Al Lulu Hospital. As usual, I have a habit of drinking three glasses of warm water in the morning with lemon. So, the second day, when my report came in, I went to the company doctor, and he said my urine test was not proper. You have mixed water into it. I said, "Why will I mix water? I have a habit of drinking three glasses of warm water in the morning, and that may be the reason for it." The doctor asked me to repeat the test. Now, the report has become normal as I did not take warm water that day.

At Al lulu hospital, after seeing my passport and earlier Yanbu company visa, an Egyptian doctor exclaimed that the prince of Saudi Arabia is my sponsor in the visa!! I said I was working in Prince's company and that is why he is my sponsor.

In the project department we had 17 employees, 7 were

Indian, 5 Arabic, 2 Pakistani and 2 (1 American and 1 Dutch from JV partner) and 1 Filipino secretary. We were initially engaged in one plant shutdown which was in Jan 2009. Then we were assigned some projects also.

Then I took up a car driving license project, as, without a car in the gulf, you are without legs in your body. You have to buy a car otherwise there is too much spending on car rent. I had passed the computer test in one go but did not pass the practical test as it was a little difficult. We have to park a car in between two parked cars in one lane. So, we have to take a full right and full left turn of the steering wheel after locating the car in proper place. If the proper distance is not maintained, it will touch another car, meaning a marking poll and fail.

So, I started training from a car training instructor at a driving school. Paid 250 SR for training. Every Thursday we have to go to school. Wait for our turn and come back. Going and coming was through rental cars. There were 2 people from our building, so I had company. Wait for 2 hours, then our turn will come, and we get one chance to drive the car. Many Pakistani, Indian and Filipino people come there for a license. Locals are hardly seen as they learn fast at early age. The instructors were Egyptians and had very short tempers. If we make mistakes, they beat us with two fingers. My American boss, who was staying in Bahrain, said if you come to Bahrain and took the test, you would easily pass the car test. He wanted me to get a license from Bahrain. On the third attempt I passed. After 10 days of attendance, we can take a retest.

After getting my driver's license, I started looking for a car for purchase. Finally, I decided to purchase a 2007 model EPICA Chevrolet car. By the look it was looking less used and as good as a new car. I purchased it for 26000 SAR. American car is so well built, sturdy and at high speed vibration was minimum. After purchase I found that AC was not sufficient. So, I took it to the mechanic and it cost me 29000 SAR Total cost of car.

In Saudi, car transfer rules are also very different. Both buyer and seller have to deposit the car and papers like iqama, driving license and car papers at the agent's office. We have to pay fees for car ownership, car insurance and agent fees. After two or three days the car will be transferred to my name and then only, I can drive.

We had a canteen in the company. We have to take a salad as per our choice. There are so many green vegetables like jarjir, bagal, parsley, carrot, cucumber, radish, radish leaf, white onion, olives etc. Then we can take rice and biryani, as we choose and pay the bills according to our selected items. There was a mechanized belt conveyor on one side of the wall, so after lunch was over, we had to put our dish on it. It will go automatically to the washing area. In the office, I used to go to my friend U's office after lunch. He was seated with one Arabic engineer. I ate chicken biryani. So, a big burping sound came from my mouth. The Saudi engineer got angry. He said this is not allowed in my culture, and he will complain against me to our boss. I said sorry, this was a natural call. I didn't know that this was considered bad. Burping, farting and standing urination are not considered good habits in the gulf.

In office I was given projects in CA plant shutdown and major modifications were to be done. like piling, coating, caustic header replacement, etc. I was handling a caustic header replacement project. I was working with one Dutch engineer. Shutdown in India is called (T&I) turn around and inspection in gulf, shutdown is unplanned shutdown whereas T&I is planned shutdown.

During Ramadan the canteen was closed so we had to make our food from home and eat in the pantry room with the door closed. Night was very lively during Ramadan. Also, it was point of get together as friends from other department also come to take lunch with us as they were single in the department.

Such a one friend from my ex-company was KJ who joined me in the same company at Vadodara in 1984. Then he moved to another complex of the company and from there he moved to Qatar. Now again in Al Jubail in my same company, so the world is round and sometimes we meet our old friends accidentally. We sang one song in 1985 in a management trainee presents program when we joined as management trainee in petrochemical company. The song was " Hututu tu jami ramta ni rutu " in english meaning in this world we all are playing the game hututu (kabbadi) from the Guajarati film Upar gagan vishal sung by great singer Manna Dey. I remembered my friend KJ especially because he is no more now and expired before 3 years with some chronic disease.

Once there was Mohamed Rafi night at Al Jubail arranged by an Indian group and many singers came from Dammam and AL Jubail. It was arranged at one of the beach camps of company. I also took part and sang the hardest song of Mohamed Rafi "O Duniya ke rakhwale sun dard bhare mere nale" from the film 'Baiju Bawra.' The song was liked by many. Even my friend KJ told you are the best singer as he was also one of singer. One other gentleman told me he came to hear this type of song only. It was a very successful and enjoyable program. My name was suggested to program organizer by KJ as he knows me as singer. When I resigned KJ told other friends that Mohamed Rafi is leaving Al jubail.

One year passed with much new learning and enthusiasm and happiness under the American management. Whenever we go to our American manager, he gives solution to it and stood behind us when we need his support. But in the second year, one new manager came from another department, and our bad days started. He was American passport holder with Pakistan origin. Shouting and firing was a usual thing. And he was shouting my name from his office many times to scare us. One new project came at that time for the replacement of six exchangers (4 tube bundles and 2 completely new heat exchangers) in the ethylene plant shutdown, which was after 6 months. It was assigned to me. A Dutch engineer was handling it, but he handed it over to me. He called me and asked. Are you sleeping at night peacefully? I replied yes. He said, "From tomorrow onwards, you will not be able to sleep because of this project." Six months was a very short time to procure six exchangers. PO procedure itself takes one month, and management approval for funds also takes some time weeks to get funds approval; but we worked 7 days a week and made it within a short time.

The new manager took me to a vendor's shop for a meeting. We arranged an urgent meeting with all the vendors and asked for a price quotation within one week. He also warned me that if I don't complete this project in six months, I will be fired. I said, "Ok, thank you." We had to give purchase order on a war footing basis as six months was too short. The company where we went had the majority of its employees from Pakistan. So, being of Pakistan origin, he was asking them how Pakistan is now. One of the employees replied in Hindi, "Saab India walone pani chhod diya." (Sir, India released water from dams, so Pakistan is submerged under water! Now as I was with him he became defensive and said India may be having problem.)

Finally, we could release PO on local company in Al Jubail and follow up on a daily basis. Daily, I had to go to the company and discuss the progress with the company representative. Finally, we got exchangers on the first day of the shutdown start date. When we installed the tube bundle and started tube side hydro testing, all the floating head covers started leaking. We called the manufacturer, and they gave us one crew for the day and another crew for the night, they tried rigorously to make the floating head straight by torch heating, and finally, they got it corrected. But those days were very stressful for me. As in the shutdown meeting, this project was shown on a critical path, which means it can delay the shutdown period, and my manager may fire me. Whenever a manufacturer company representative came, and management asked him whether he would be able to complete this job, his only answer was Insha'Allah. And again, the question repeated, and again, the answer was the same. Even Saudi engineers started repeating his answer with smile. Finally, we could complete the project within time and me and my management got relieved from tension.

One of our colleagues, B, resigned as he was very much

upset with new manager. He sent his family to India and came back and resigned. His farewell party was arranged in a five-star hotel in Ramadan tent. All department personnel came, including the manager. All gave farewell speech with some memory. B came in Arabic attire. Meanwhile, the new manager was also given a pink slip by management, which is why he was also somewhat depressed. Because he ran a department in autocratic management style, all the employee, Arabic, western and Indian, were unhappy with him. At the farewell party I sang one song of Mohamed Rafi "Chal udja re panchhi ke ab ye desh hua begana" from film Bhabhi means "O bird fly away now this country is not suitable for you to reside." It was so touchy that new manager started weeping. Arabic engineers were also greatly surprised at the effect of the song.

Now that manager was very much happy with me. He even started talking with me in my mother tongue Gujarati. My Indian friend was also very surprised. He was asking me which language you were talking I replied our mother tongue Gujarati. He gave me a very good rating as I completed exchanger replacement project within time and cost.

When we were going to the office, on the way I told my colleague B that I am also in a process of resigning. I thought I will handover you my workload but you resigned first so I have to take your charge. He said no, you are lying, you will not resign. I said once my visa is received, I will resign. But he did not believe me. Another colleague, N, then said no, no when Rajen said there must be some stuff. He will not tell lie. He openly took my side and supported me. Even though both were from same state West Bengal.

Actually, I was contacted by one manpower supply company to depute me in one oil and gas company in Bahrain on a contract basis with 6000 USD monthly fix pay. However, I was not ready to go again on contract employee status from a direct hire company employee in Saudi Arabia. Also, in two years I could win the confidence of management that I can handle any difficult project and can complete it within cost and time. So, I contacted the company and asked them if they wanted me to take on as a direct hire employee. They agreed and took my telephonic interview, and selected. I gave an interview on roadside seating as in my house, a clear mobile signal was not coming. Then, the company asked me to visit Bahrain for a personal interview and medical test.

At that time, in Saudi, Thursday and Friday were holidays, and in Bahrain, Friday and Saturday, so I fixed to come on Wednesday evening and give medical and personal interviews on Thursday. My family was also with me on vacation, so I asked the HR person whether I could bring my family to Bahrain. He agreed that no problem if you can come, we will give you a bigger room in the guest house. At the guest house at reception, they gave me a small carpet; I asked what this was. They replied that it was for prayer. Yes, in gulf prayer is the most important and prayer room is part of every building malls and offices.

Thursday, I went to the engineering department office, the behaviour and manners of my superintendent was so good that it attracted me to join Bahrain. He took me to all the members of the department, including managers, and introduced me as I was joining the company as an area engineer for one complex. Salary negotiation was done and when I got expected salary, I accepted the offer.

Finally, we went back to Saudi on Thursday night. Then I booked air ticket for my daughter and wife as my daughter had passed the 12 th science exam and was supposed to get admission into medicine. When I went to drop them off at the airport, the Immigration officer said your visa was not showing in the system because it was an exit re-entry type visa, so you consumed it. Then it clicked in my mind that I thought family also had multiple visas, but that was only in my passport. For them, I have to get a visa again. So, we went back from Dammam airport to Al Jubail. After getting a new exit visa, they could go to India after one week.

My new Saudi manager took my four times exit interviews and only one question was asked. What can they do to stop me going? I replied now I have decided to go so there is no looking back. Thank you very much for your feeling. Four times I was interviewed by my manager and one time by the general manager.

Company arranged my farewell at the company beach camp. They ordered three big dishes filled with biryani rice and dry fruits and nuts. And big roasted white sheep sitting on it. On one dish we Indian joined, another was occupied by Saudi employees and third was by Filipinos.

Initially, they gave a short speech, including my Dutch engineer colleague. He praised me for my negotiation skills in addition to technical expertise. Because I saved money on one project by negotiating with a contractor. Technically, my American manager and Dutch engineer also experienced my knowledge, and I could earn their confidence in me. The general manager also appreciated my work and told me to consider the company as my home, and that any time I wanted to come back, I could come back, and they would be happy to take me in. I received their love and respect, which I could not get in India even after serving 22 years!!!

I had another strange experience at Al Jubail. We shifted to a new building as the old building had no proper sunlight or air. It was like an underground house where no sunlight or air could come. The new house was on the road and had new wide windows, tiles, bathrooms and toilets. So, we were very happy to stay there as we could see all the cars coming and going from the kitchen. The other bedroom side also has very good aluminium sliding windows. Within 15 days, a local man came from a nearby building and told us that we needed to cover half of our windows with aluminium sheets, and that would be arranged by him so that we cannot see thru. He came with a carpenter. He took dimensions and fitted them within week, and we were back to square one. We could not argue much as it is their country and culture we have to obey!!!

In Saudi I felt that I am in foreign land, so it prompted me to keep on searching for a free country.

Bahrain experience:

As you start earning money, you try to move to a free country where you can stay freely without fear of religious police. So, when we were doing a job in Saudi Arabia, there was a feeling that if we got a job in Bahrain Oman or UAE, we would be fortunate. Manpower always tries to shift to higher salary, better living conditions, freedom, and permanent residency. This is the main reason for migrating to European countries, and America, and Canada, and Australia. If you earn money and cannot enjoy it, it is like adding zero to numbers only.

Bahrain is a very expat friendly country, and people respect expatriates and like Indians. Bahrain is a country of birds, beaches and hotels. If you come from Saudi Arabia, it feels better than coming from India. If you see both ends, you can feel the difference. After crossing causeway between Saudi to Bahrain you feel like you are coming from closed life to open life, with full of freedom in Bahrain. You can pass time on beaches or bars as per your choice. When we were coming to Bahrain from Saudi Arabia, we generally stayed in hotels near Manama. There are many good hotels near Gold Souk and Juffair. As soon as we pass the Causeway Bridge and enter Bahrain, one fresh feeling of freedom goes deep in our breath.

Initially they gave me bachelor accommodation in company township. Township was very goog planned with wide road and compounded villas with all around haze and gardening and sitting space. It was designed and created by American company so with wooden houses same as USA. After a two-month stay in the company township at a bachelor's house, I moved to east Riffa on the main market road. I was staying in east Riffa, from there my company was just 4 km away from my residence. There were 4 Indian Gujarati families staying at East Riffa. Initially, I was taken by my friend R in his car for shopping and orientation to the Company, club program and Swaminarayan temple program for Diwali and New Year. We two families were from the same city, Vadodara, while the other two were from Surat city.

In our company, there were 200 Indian families. Indians were from, all corners of India, i.e. south, north, east and west. In some of the national day celebration, like 15 August and 26 January, we celebrated together. Other regional festivals like kite festival (Makar Sankranti), Diwali and Holi.

Many cultural programs were celebrated by a Gujarati group led by R who was staying in our building. We all were working hand in hand and there will be many sub committees like music committee, food committee, account committee, etc. earlier only 500 to 700 were total attendees but as the new project came many Guajarati operators arrived from Gujarat and we had to change the location from one place to big hall where 1000 can attend the cultural celebration.

Kite festivals are generally arranged in tents during the winter season. Around 14 January generally with Friday keeping in mind kite flying date was fixed so maximum member can attend. The kites are brought from India, and managing them requires very minute management. The person who is coming from India will bring some kites and strings in their luggage, and that way, booking and bringing from India will be arranged. The tent will be booked for 24 hours, so from morning to evening, Bahrain residents will enjoy, but those who were coming from Saudi will leave the next day morning. So, they will stay the night in tents.

Breakfast, lunch, and dinner were ordered from one caterer earlier. K was very enthusiastic about giving this service and providing it at very competitive rates. It was like an ARC annual rate contract. But he got cancer, went to India, and died there. It was very shocking news as we ate his food for many years. Sometimes, he would run for water, bread, and other things when a shortage occurred during the Friday and Saturday holidays, but overall, the experience was very good with him.

Indian groups were initially celebrating all major common festivals like 15 August Indian Independence Day and 26 January Indian republic day. All Indians will celebrate with cultural and patriotic songs. I was taking part in singing as it was my hobby. My favourite song of Mohamed Rafi "Kar chale hum fida jan tan sathiyo ab tumhare hawale vatan sathio" means soldier says we are leaving this world by sacrificing ourselves and now this country is your responsibility, a last wish of a soldier was liked by my friends. I sang this song during kargil war at two places in India and got first prize. Now many veteran Indians retired and their kids also grew up so now these programs are not arranged but it was history.

There was an election for president of the cricket club in our company township at Bahrain. Two groups were there, eastern and western. Our Indian friend did a lot of canvassing and increased the Indians' membership in the cricket club. We all attended that meeting on election days. Finally, Indian president was declared winner and it was so celebrating day that we all went to cricket club bar and enjoyed victory with chilled beer. Scenario was similar to winning of the Indian cricket team in the film Lagaan by Aamir khan.

My Turkish boss was knowing more about India thru election of parent committee as his children were studying in Indian school. He was saying how Indian sub group forms in election. North India versus south India, Kerala versus rest of India etc. In one party he told south Indian superintendent that see your engineers are drinking soda if my Gujju engineers were there they will drink costliest wine because they know value of money! He was asking us to bring Chivas regal whiskey from air port duty free as price was 3 times more in Bahrain. It was used in team building events held at farmhouse and hotels.

I stayed 7 years in East Riffa. East Riffa is just 10 minutes away from my company and looks more like a small town than a city. On Friday and Saturday, labour comes from nearby camps; otherwise, it is not as crowded as Manama. In 2011, but there was no drainage system in the Riffa. Vacuum Tankers used to come to collect waste from the underground tank in all buildings, and if it doesn't come, it will overflow. Sometimes, we thought of leaving Riffa due to car parking problem and drainage overflow, but the bonding of our 4 family was so strong that nobody thought to go.

I had a walking friend P who also liked walking too much. We used to walk in different gardens and on street roads. Also, on the market road, many shops come, which gives us a chance to visit different shops daily. Like the grocery shop, garment, scent, dates, gold, specs, Arabic sweet shops, barber, mobile accessories shop, etc. Karak tea and chicken shawarma shop at intervals of every ten shops. There are abaya shops, dress material shops and gift shops. Date balance selling persons were many who extend the date validity of the sim card and recharge balance of the sim card. Generally, they stand on the road, Mostly Bangladeshis are doing this job. There were three gardens, namely Khalifa Al kubra Garden, Riffa Garden and one on the way to West Riffa on the downside road Hunainiyah public park.

After East Riffa I moved to Tubli in 2019 on the sea shore near Manama as my walking partner friend P moved there in the last 1 year and I was alone in Riffa. Without partner it is difficult to maintain a daily walking schedule. During sweating summer, it was a challenge to walk on roads. But we walked. It took 1 year to move to Tubli because I wanted flat with balcony and finally I got three balconies with each room.

In Tubli, there were many places to walk on the seashore from our residence to the Sitra fly-over bridge. About 3 km long road with wide place for walking as no shops like Riffa and without any heavy traffic. Friday, we walked to Tubli town, purchase some vegetables from the mall, and drink coffee at roadside restaurants. On Friday Saturday at 6 am, we have a good morning message on mobile from whosoever awake first, and at 7 am, we start walking. In the evening, we went to the seashore at Tubli and check the sea level, there was a small boat dock station, and wooden poll markings were there to measure low tide and high tide.

About six feet was the difference. Fishermen generally fill the fuel and start fishing in the nearby sea. Observing high tide and low tide, seagull birds every morning meet at the seashore in big numbers near Sitra over bridge as if they have an annual general body meeting AGM of company shareholders! During lowest tide, Filipino people come with buckets and stools and go into the sea. Seat on a stool as the water level is hardly one foot. They catch crabs and clams. The crab of Bahrain is exported to Korea and a favourite dish is made from it in Korea. Some times for change we go to sea shore in morning on Friday to see high tides. In ground at a time we saw 3 different expat teams were playing cricket. Gulf national game is football.

After spending 4 years at Tubli and in the vicinity of the sea, I moved to a company township in the southern governorate in 2023, because of heavy traffic while going and coming back from the company. It was 19 km, and there were many signals. In the morning, school timing coincided with office timing, so on either side, there was heavy traffic; My residence and company location were like on circle so from both side of circle we can go to office, but unfortunately there were schools on both alternate route so we have to suffer from heavy traffic. Big SUVs with a parent and one child are normal on the road, which increases traffic. Unlike India, Bahrain's local people don't believe in carpooling, i.e. One parent daily takes 4 children on a turn-by-turn basis and drops them at school, which can save petrol and reduce traffic also. Alternatively, to reduce traffic problem my company started flexi-time, so in the morning, between 6 and 8.30 am, we can clock in, and after counting 8.30 hrs duty, we can clock out.

The company town ship is 80 years old and was built by an American company for their employees who came to Bahrain for oil exploration and later refinery operation. Wide roads with amenities like a garden, hospital, swimming pool, cricket ground, football ground, tennis court, club, bar, etc., make it an ideal place to live. But a lonely place for bachelors. Houses are also made in American style, i.e., timber-built with wooden flooring. And with a garden and walking space. As it is away from city traffic, going to the office is peaceful, without many traffic signals or traffic jams passing thru oil fields seeing oil wells donkey pump doing their job. Date trees and babul trees are many in the township. Birds are also many and if you give feed daily about 100 birds are visiting my neighbour's house. And as birds come, cats also follow them to catch their prey. Now we have also started feeding birds with feed and water. on outside house wall on light bulb bird have built nests and yearly bird comes to put their eggs in winter.

Many trees are also grown by me in my house garden in the township, I planted Tamarind tree, Neem tree (Azadirachta Indica), Sweet neem tree, which is generally in

India used as spices, Gunda tree (Glue berry), Indian cork tree (Malingtonia), Moringa tree (Miracle tree/drumstick tree), Jungle jalebi tree (Madras thorn) jujube tree, guava tree, champa (Plumeria) tree, jamun tree some creepers like Rangoon creeper, aparajita, jui and many more. I already had grown trees in the pot at Tubli, which I transferred to soil in the town ship, and many have grown to full height, like 6 to 10 feet. Tamarind word was given by Arabs when they came to India for trading in ancient time they saw tamarind so named it tamar Alhind India's date as inner part of fruit looks like date khajur. Then it became tamarind world wide. in ancient time there were Ibn Battuta and Albiruni who traveled to India and wrote book on it. now there is Ibn Battuta mall in Dubai and Albaironi company name in KSA given to remember these great travelers. There is tradition of keeping company name on great Arab scientist in KSA like Ibn Sina, Ibn Rushd, Ibn Zahr, etc.

Some plants are still in the pot like gardenia, bougainvillea, money plant, etc.

Being an environmentalist, I started distributing seeds to my friends. I have distributed to many of my friends moringa seedlings and seeds in the township. One friend asked me what is the benefit to me why I am distributing? I replied I will get oxygen generated from it. When some friend bring moringa sticks and gives me saying this fruit is of moringa tree grown from your seeds which you gave me. Some sends me photograph of tree also and says so many birds are staying in it, I feel happy and satisfied. I have also taken part in mangrove plantation at sea shore and beach clean-up drive sponsored by my company. Also, I am a member of oil spill in which, in case of oil spill in sea water, our job is to collect, store, transport and dispose oil at disposal site.

I have also made some slogans to promote awareness about tree plantation and environment among children.

1. Seeds are for growing and not for throwing.

2. Trees are our forefathers, we exist because tree exist.

3. We are dependent on trees for oxygen, they are not.

4. Grow one tree and return oxygen you have taken as loan from mother earth.

Chapter

6

Gulf Hobbies

Cars: In India we have various mode of transport like public bus, van, rickshaw, taxi metro train etc. There is no public transport available in the Gulf like the metro trains except in Dubai and Qatar. Cars, taxi and bus are the only mode of transport here. One of my Arabic friends told me that Indians are spending on the education of their children, and Arabic people spend on mobile phones and cars. Cars are a very favourite item here, and Arabic people are very much fond of cars and driving. Toyota is the market leader (about 40% share) in the Gulf. Arabic people like to have SUVs, big vehicles with 7-seater capacity and 2,5 cc engines and above. Due to family size, they also have to purchase a 7-seater with 5 children, and the husband and wife become 7, which is a normal family size in the gulf. We had in our company one employee in Bahrain who had 11 children.

When I went to Saudi in 2007, women were not allowed to drive. So, either hired drivers or Saudi kids were driving at a very early age, so by the time they become eligible to drive, they become masters in driving. Sometimes, they have to bring drivers from India. Also, car drifting is a very popular but risky game for Saudi youths. They run a car with speed, and then they change direction by U-turn. Many videos of car drifting are available on social media. Even a video is there where a Saudi youth changed tyres while driving a tilting car and driving one side of wheels.

Sometimes some youth lost their lives. In the office When we drive car and go with Saudi colleagues to visit nearby plants, in return they will not allow us to drive. They say we Indians drive very slowly and with fear. They take keys from us. They drive like they are born drivers. With speed they will take it to the parking area and stop at the right place with a break, even at high speed also they have very good control on driving.

We have travelled many times when Saudi taxi drivers put their legs on top of the seat, put the car on cruise control and drink coffee with full pleasure.

Toyota Prado and Camry are the most popular models in gulf. GMC Yukon and Tahoe are also very popular SUV models. Indian expats initially mostly buy Toyota Corolla, Nissan Sunny, and Honda City. As time pass and become senior like 10 years and above, they start thinking about SUVs selling sedan cars. All car models, from Porsche to Maserati, are seen on the roads.

When my son came to Bahrain for the first time, he did not see these many cars in India. He exclaimed. My nephew S said he did not see a car with L marks. I informed him that it is a Lexus of TOYOTA Japan which is not launched in India as it is a premium car. In Saudi I had purchased a Chevrolet Epica. It was a very nice car. It was an American car well-built sturdy and even at 100 kilometre per hour it was not giving any vibration problem.

When I came to Bahrain, I had to sell my Saudi car, Epica Chevrolet, as in Saudi, you have to sell the car and pay all dues before applying for a final exit visa. Wanted to purchase a Toyota Corolla. So, I saw many cars but finally landed on Nissan Sunny model 2011, which was 6 months old and had a 1000 BHD discount. I purchased it at 5100 BHD. Up to 2017, I ran it and initially learned to drive in narrow roads and round about rules of Bahrain. Small cars are better as roads in Bahrain are narrower than in Saudi Arabia, and roundabouts were a new thing for me. Also, initially coming from India, our spending capacity was low. As we stay more and more years in the gulf, our heart capacity in cc also expands and becomes more, and we try to purchase higher cc cars with large capacity SUVs like locals.

The Gulf car market is flooded as all car companies and all models of world-leader manufacturers are available. From cheap to premium cars like BMW, Mercedes, Range Rover, Porsche, etc. There is a very big second-hand car market. On every road, you will find a big car showroom for second-hand cars, and very good cars can be purchased at a very low price. For selling and purchasing car and household items, expatriates.com is a very useful website. Even premium cars like Mercedes and BMW are also available at very low prices, which we cannot even imagine purchasing in India. Only cricketers and film stars can purchase in India.

I purchased a BMW X5 2008 white model at 4100 dinars in Bahrain in 2017. It was an SUV with a 4.8 litre capacity engine with 8 cylinders and 97000 km run. I purchased it from a Chinese lady who was transferred to Dubai and wanted to sell it. I saw her car on the expatriates.com website. But the price was high so I just called her. In the advertisement, she said the price was 5200 BD. When I called her, she gave me a price of 4500 BD. Then I told her my price was 4000 BD. She gave me a trial drive. I liked the car. Then I also forgot, and after one and half months, I found on expatriate.com again her advertisement. I asked her whether the car was still available. She said yes. I told her my price was 4000 BD. Then she slowly came down, and I came somewhat up as I liked it. Before that, I carried out a computer test and repair cost, so it had a repair cost of 1500 BD, mainly for tyre replacement.

My basis for purchasing a premium car is I have only 2 to 3 years remaining for retirement, and in India, I cannot purchase an X5 car for 3 reasons. The car price is very high, about 1 crore INR, and the petrol price is also very high in India 100 INR per litre, about 4 times. Road conditions are also not suitable for this type of premium car as it is good at high speed, which is difficult to drive in India. In the city area, you can hardly drive above 50 kmph. These cars, generally in the Gulf, are used by rich sheikhs who purchase these cars and replace them after a 5-year warranty period as the maintenance costs are high due to spare part costs. For up to five years, they have a free maintenance contract from the car company. I had experience with American, Japanese, Korean and Indian cars, but I did not drive German cars, so I thought this was the right time for me to go for a German car BMW. It is a very premium car brand name, like Mercedes, Range rover and it will be a new trend in my Indian group. Even if I spend another 4000 BD, then it also costs me 8100 BD, which is half the price of the Toyota Prado that some of my friends purchased.

And that is exactly what I thought was a big mind changer for all our Indian friends. My one friend told me he was looking at me daily, visiting the expatriate.com website for the X5 model, but didn't think I would buy it. Another friend told you have made history. Until now, people thought the Toyota Prado was the ultimate choice Indians could think of. You have thought one step ahead, and now, we can think about premium cars like BMW, Range rover and Mercedes. Even my Turkish boss couldn't digest it, and he asked me in every department weekly meeting whether I sold BMW or not? He thought I would sell it due to the high maintenance cost. Finally I had to reply him that after 3 years I will retire and sell you at half price, then he stopped. After shared my photo with X5 on Face book, when I went to India, one of my ex-bosses from my previous company told me congratulations!!! Then he asked, "Do you know for what?" I replied for BMW X5? He said yes.

When I went to the Gujarati social gathering, one friend commented that the car owner might not be our company employee. When he knew I had purchased it, he said now you will be known as BMW Wala. Many friends expressed their desire to have a test drive and I was offering it freely as I wanted to expand my BMW X5 club. One friend on the verge of taking it finally purchased Prado. One English friend also purchased an X5 at a very cheap price, about the price of 1200 BD. But still, he was happy, and that is the value of German cars. Very sturdy. Even a 10-year-old car looks like 5 years old. Also, in German cars, all features were world-class, like sturdy design, maximum safety, cruise control, leather seats, camera, sensor, seat adjustment, and panoramic roof with the best music system.

I had to change all the tyres of my X5 to make it really safe at the cost of 520 BD as it was run-flat tyre, which is less thick than normal tyre and can last about 50 kilometres even if it has punctured. Also, there were American, European, Korean and Chinese brand tyres, and the cost will change per country. Earlier tyres were Chinese tyres in X5 which were old, and whenever they were met with pointed stones, a big chunk of part would come out. So, I felt I spent money purchasing a safe car, and if I didn't replace the tyres, it was not safe at all. I even gave a lecture on tyre safety in my company as a part of a departmental safety meeting that we engineer had to conduct. One time, I had to take my X5 car to the garage urgently as the handbrake got stuck. It cost me 500 BD, which I came to realize that maintenance cost is a costly factor, and that is why local and expatriate people don't purchase German cars.

One of my friends, B, just purchased X5, looking at my justification that now we are old people and we should see safety as a prime factor. He purchased it and, after 6 months, met with an accident. One Saudi driver touched his car and my friend turned his car in fear which hit with wall. But he did not get any scars. He exclaimed that due to X5 only, he was saved. After getting money from insurance he again purchased a X5. This has doubled my confidence and satisfaction that my choice was right.

I was interested in purchasing the X5, but my confidence was increased when I got push from one of my friends, S, who was purchasing premium cars like BMW, Lexus and Mercedes only. He was clearly telling us that if you want to purchase second-hand premium cars, then only come to me for guidance; if you want a new car, then don't come to me. He said he purchased all the premium cars such as BMW cars, and now he has a Mercedes SUV. He was sending us daily "car for sale" advertisements from his own sources like OLX, etc. With different models and prices, we saw real enthusiasm in him and a passion for premium cars. So, I decided to go for premium cars after seeing him. He had contacts with many agents also. He will even come to see the vehicles with us. At present, he has a BMW bike also.

Second-hand used cars are so popular and available that you can purchase them from branded car showrooms. Renowned companies themselves offer second-hand used cars. With the model, price, and kilometres driven, all cars are kept in good condition. Some agents are selling second-hand cars. Even some garages import cars from Europe and sell them with all the historical details like kilometres run, model year and accident history. For new car purchases, Ramadan is the best time as during that time, interest rates are lower, and some kind of discount is also available on new car purchases. However, Toyota is an exception as they are always in demand, so trial drives are also not offered. Forget about discount. Now government site Bahrain.bh gives complete accident history and owner change record of car.

Talking on mobile while driving is a big problem in Bahrain, mainly women driver in Bahrain. One day my, friend P were coming back from putting my car in the garage for repairs. One lady came with fast speed while talking on the phone. We stopped because one pedestrian was crossing the road and he pressed the signal light to red to cross roads. She banged from the back of my friend's car. My friend and I was seeing in rear camera that she is rushing with speed while talking on mobile and we felt helplessly will bang and finally she banged. Immediately she called her relative. we went to traffic police and police prepared papers for insurance.

Hookah Bar:

This is a very famous Arabic tradition. Many of men and women are habituated for shisha or Hubble bubbles. Smoking is very common in the Gulf, and all cigarette companies make money like anything. Now, the government has raised taxes on cigarettes in line with liquor, so some friends recommend bringing cigarettes along with from duty-free shop from airport. In Saudi, my house owner was 80 years old, but he kept one Bengali boy as his caretaker. Daily, he will take him to a hookah bar for smoking. Many varieties of hookah are available in shops, and they are very attractive. In shops also, one-hand pipe and in one-hand mobile is common in hookah bars. Also, they like football matches, so they will also be screened on big-wall TV in hukkah bar. Sitting on a Majlis sofa with legs straightened on the floor. The hookah is normally seen here at many places. I have seen local women smoking shisha on the beach. Now e cigarette or vape also become popular in the gulf which is banned in India.

Wine bar and dance bars:

All five-star hotels in Bahrain have wine bars and dance bars.

Belly dance is popular in the Arab world. Many visitors from Saudi Arabia come to Bahrain on Fridays and Saturdays for drinks and dance. It is like Daman, Diu and Mount Abu for Gujarat people as Gujarat is a dry state in India; the hotel industry depends on visitors from Gujarat in Diu, Daman and Mount Abu. Similarly, as the majority of lonely expats live in the gulf, they come to Bahrain for drink as it is banned in KSA and spend time in the bars during weekends. And all Bahrain hotels remain house full during weekends.

Perfume and Scent shops:

In the Gulf market, every 10 shops, you can find one perfume shop and one sweet and chocolate. There are many scent shops in the gulf, and from 1 BD to 50 BD per bottle, you can see. Many costly brands are also available as all local people, men and women, invariably use scent. Arabic lady uses more scent than men. Maybe in the Gulf, humidity is very high during the six months of summer, and to suppress the smell of human sweat, consumption of scent is too much. All major perfume manufacturers have branches in the Gulf. Oud is a favourite flavour of Arabic people. It is a costly flavour but is liked in the Gulf the most. When I went to visit Kerala in India, I saw an Oud tree plantation project being implemented there in the forest with the help of Saudi aid.

Chapter 7

Other Countries Experiences Shared By Friends

Qatar: Qatar is almost an island country connected with Saudi by land; the area is more than Bahrain. Also, it is a rich country due to vast gas resources. Qatar have established country-wise gas supply trains to supply liquified natural gas LNG for a 25-year long-term contract. Qatar hosted an international game event, the FIFA World Cup, in 2022. This shows they can arrange such a big show. For this event, they had hotel accommodation shortages, so hired cruise ships for that period and kept them in the sea as floating hotels.

Qatar is a good paymaster so it is also a good destination to go for oil and gas jobs. Many of my friends are serving there and happily living as it is rich in gas, like Saudi is rich in oil reserves. Bahrain has not that much oil production like Saudi and gas production like Qatar. Whenever we go for walk in interview at Mumbai, we saw huge crowd of candidate appearing for it. I lost three chances of Qatar jobs, one at Vadodara where I gave interview and did not get selected another time when landed at Saudi and I got call from them and third time I was short listed but could not attend due to miscommunication of agent.

Oman: Oman is also considered as good as Bahrain in the freedom point of view for expats. It is a big country and its proximity to Dubai attracts people to go there for jobs and business. For drink we have to take a license in Oman. Alcohol is not free like Bahrain where no license required you can buy liquor in shops or online from big stores like BMMI. I had got opportunity for Oman but as I already submitted my papers for Saudi visa, I declined it. The interviewer was advising me why you are going to Saudi it is like golden cage. In Oman you will feel freedom same like India.

Abu Dhabi:

Abu Dhabi is also rich in petroleum and has a big oil company where my friends are working. They have a very good township at Ruwais about 150 km away from Abu Dhabi. Daily to and from travel is long, so everyone has to purchase a SUV car only. Many friends have changed their job in other countries because of long-distance travel. Yes, it is in proximity to Dubai, so you can visit Dubai frequently.

Dubai:

Dubai is the most developed city and has all the qualities of smart city. It has good road, metro and bus facility. The tallest tower of the world Burj Khalifa is situated here as shown in my book front page. Dubai is the most cosmopolitan and has attracted businessmen from all the corners of the world. Population wise Indian are maximum 37% followed by

Pakistan, Bangladesh and Philippines. Dubai local population is only 10 % rest all are expats. Many Indians have settled in Dubai as businessmen and expanded their businesses to other gulf countries, such as the Lulu Mall which has more than 100 malls in the gulf. My Saudi friend told me he has seen many Indians living in Dubai in such a big villas which he cannot purchase. In Dubai every year they are adding new facilities to attract tourist from the world. you can buy villa and they give permanent residency so all big film stars from India have purchased villa in Dubai.

Chapter

8

Money Management

What are the investment options for NRI (Non-Resident Indians)?

There is a vast difference between Gulf NRI and western NRI. We call gulf NRI as half NRI because all are bound to go back to India one day. Whereas Americans, European, Canadians or Australians are never going to come back to India as they are citizens of those developed countries.

NRIs can invest in real estate like shops and commercial plots, industrial plots, companies' shares mutual funds, gold and businesses and start-ups. Oil and gas sector company jobs sometimes last longer, like many of my friends who have spent 25 years in the Gulf, and some even crossed forty years. But some unfortunates return back to India and die in one year only. So, going for a Gulf job also has risk. Many long serving NRI do not get their dream to come back to India and die in gulf itself.

Every country has localization programs to create jobs for local youths, such as Saudization, Qatarization, Bahrainization, Omanization etc. Expatriates are temporarily hired to get experienced people from around the world. Also, they recruit people from all over the world to avoid one-country dominance. In the Gulf, there is a visa quota limit per country like USA to create multi nationality culture.

Indian expat generally makes all investment in India. Filipino expats generally live lavish life and spend more than saving. If you ask them are you doing saving, they will ask counter question for what? English people migrate to Thailand as standard of living, cost of house and income tax is less. Pakistani expats are generally either stay in gulf permanently by applying golden visa or migrate to Canada and USA where their children are staying. Venezuelan expat generally don't want to go back to Venezuela due to poor law and order and high inflation they will either migrate to Europe as they have dual passport. Bangladeshi send money to Bangladesh and help relatives to start business or shops.

Investment is the major factor in the gulf; if you earn and don't invest in good manners, your money will start to decrease, and at the end, you will see no good return on investment (ROI) as per your wish. If properly invested, then only retirement life becomes stress-free; otherwise, many NRIs get complete funds wiped out due to bad decisions. One of my Indian friends lost heavily as he invested in a partnership with his cousin's in the electronics business, and the cousin cheated him. He was like back to ground zero as he sold all his property in India and repaid liabilities. Fortunately, he could bounce back. And now, again he opened Filipino restaurant, he is doing well. Some foreigners lose their jobs and are not allowed to leave the country as they cannot repay the loan taken from the bank. In this condition, they are forced to work in low-level jobs.

1.   Shares and mutual fund investment

Shares and mutual funds are the best option for NRIs. Many banks provide online share trading apps along with NRI accounts, which facilitate online trading from the Gulf. Technology has changed business rules, such as online trading. Many employees work from home also. To increase working hours, almost all companies provide laptops to their employees. During covid, many employees of the gulf were working from home in India due to travel restrictions.

There are two types of investors in shares. One who watches, studies, analyses and purchases shares on a long-term basis. There are technical and fundamental analysis approaches for the prediction of the share price. One should study before investing and take any one of them or a combination of these analysis. Fundamental analysis is based on the intrinsic value of company assets, whereas technical analysis is a graphical analysis of share prices and predicts future trends. Some investors are doing daily basis purchases and selling, which is called intraday trading. Some are doing purchase on hearsay and sell in panicky they make loss in share market. If you can watch on a daily-basis shares online, intraday trading is good, but if you want peace of mind and don't have analytical power and study and don't want to see daily basis share prices and increase or decrease your blood pressure, it is better to go for mutual funds.

There is my simple rule of investment in shares: every five to seven years there is an up and down cycle in the stock market or index. When the index is low and you have surplus money invest in A grade shares, and when the index is high sell it off. You will make profit without any much risk provided you must have holding-power for 5-7 years. During covid time 2019 market was very low. now in 2024 it has upper cycle so, who purchased shares of A grade during covid now making lot of money. One must remember the rule of investment high risk high returns.

2.   Real estate investment

Real estate in metro cities are having good ROI on rent and asset value. but in small cities like Vadodara, it is very less compared to capital cost. One of my friends has purchased properties in Bangalore as rent is highest there due to IT companies. One of my friends purchased 2 BHK apartment in Mumbai at Rs 55 lacs before 20 years now its cost is increased to 2.5 Crore and rent, he is getting is INR 50,000 per month.

Also rent of shops and houses are falling down and municipal tax and society maintenance charge increases if you give property on rent, at the end hardly 5 percent return, we are getting in comparison to mutual funds which give 10 to 15 percent interest which is quite attractive.

It is not that all money should be invested in one option. From time to time one sector becomes shining and another becomes weak so investment should be done in a balanced manner and as the rule of investment says all the eggs should not be put in one basket.

3. Gold investment

Gold investment also proves better as in recent times it has gone up, so if you make systematic investments in all these commodities in a diversified manner, there are chances of averaging, and you get an average 10 per cent return easily. Gold is considered the strongest among all investments, and in case of war and calamities, it can only give good returns. Before 10 years, it remained flat as the price did not rise, but recently, there has been a tremendous rise in gold prices. Indian women have the highest affinity towards gold in the world and they always try to purchase every year basis SIP! Maximum gold is reserved in India in the form of jewellery.

4. Foreign Currency Investment

In the Gulf, you have the opportunity to invest in international funds, keep your money in dollars, and get a better return. Even some Gulf countries give the option to purchase real estate to expatriates. Now, the Bahrain government started giving golden visas, which are for 10 years. This gives the advantage of bringing family and doing business or study for son and daughter. One of my friends from Pakistan has not sent any money to Pakistan as his daughter is married and doing a job in Canada, and his son is also studying in Canada and settled there. He has taken a golden visa for himself and his wife. When he retires, his plan is to stay in Bahrain till he gets PR in Canada. His daughter can apply for a parent visa once she pays income tax for consecutive 3 years in Canada. If we didn't send any money to India as remittance now the conversion rate would have doubled in ten years so money would have doubled automatically. When I came in Bahrain it was 120 rupees per BD in 2010. Now it is 222 INR for 1 Bahrain dinar, almost double.

5.   Industry investment

Some expatriates purchase small units in industrial areas and start manufacturing.

Some have a hotel, restaurant, industry, some start school and college business. So now once you have money you can get many opportunities. Some countries offer direct citizenship if you invest the minimum required fund in those countries. USA has special EB5 visa program under which if you invest 800,000 USD you get direct green card for family.

I met one expatriate on the plane while travelling from India who was from Qatar. He told me that he had started a factory in Tanzania manufacturing copper wire from copper ore. Later on, he plans to start an electric cable factory there. He said he has one readymade garment factory at Amreli, his native place in Gujarat, India. He had dream to give employment to 100 persons from his village. One of my friends who resigned from Bahrain and went to Qatar is moving back to India to handle his milk production unit.

6. FD investment

Fixed deposit is the lowest type of investment in recent days. Hardly you get 5 to 6 % interest per year. My friends who were doing FD, and we called them FD Baba for many years, have now switched over to mutual funds. FDs are for those who want to take zero risk in investment. Or have a phobia of other investments. But remember, in economics, high risk high return, so a combination is the best idea. When you go to investment consultant, they also advise you on investment based on your age, income, liabilities and risk appetite, which means how much you want to take risks. Aggressive moderate or lowest. Accordingly, he will suggest funds to invest. Nowadays, mutual funds are the best option for those who cannot watch share pieces daily and have little knowledge of share because share price tracking, study, knowledge, and analysis is like aptitudes.

7. Other investment options

Now many countries offer citizenship if you invest minimum

prescribed amount them. People invest amount and gets family shifted there if their home country is not safe or for better life style. Also, bitcoins have become another currency for investment and its price is rising. Old paintings and wines antique items etc are investment tools. What will happen in the new age of AI nobody knows and fear is there that many professions will disappear in future.

Chapter

9

Initial Problems Faced By Expats

Food

Food is a major problem in the gulf so the first requirement is you should know cooking. In gulf south Indian restaurants and Arabic and Pakistani restaurants are many, but vegetarian restaurants are very few or none. Outside eating is fine for some days and not always. I knew how to cook. In the initial days myself and S was staying in partnerships at Yanbu. He was cooking nonveg and I was cooking veg food for us. Vegetarian who come from Gujarat have very big problem as they cannot eat in mix restaurant and pure vegetarian restaurant is rarely available in Saudi Arabia. In Yanbu there was no pure vegetarian restaurant, only two main restaurants were Pakistani.

Arabic foods are less spicy and mostly grill items and rice items like biryani so when we come from India, we are habituated with spicy food like Puna mishal, Sev usal, Vada pav and rice with dal tadka. Only rice we cannot eat so we need some gravy. In Saudi, some time I had to use American hot sauce to make rice spicy so that I could eat in company canteen. Arabic friends also afraid of Indian spicy food so first they will ask whether it is spicy. One day I brought sing bhujiya from India and given it to my local friend he gave it to his sons. Next day he was complaining which food you brought my all sons were crying for water! In English there is one saying that when you are in Rome do like romans so, eat Arabic food slowly you will love it. My Arabic friend liked lilo chevdo which is specialty of my city Vadodara which is basically potato chips. He said all taste are mixed in it, sweet, sour, hot etc.

Rental house

Finding a rental house is also a big project in Saudi, and if it is a bachelor, then it is very difficult. The family can only stay in the family building. Also, rent in Saudi is to be paid annually together in advance, so it is big money, and if we resign or go back in between, the agent will not refund it. If you find your replacement, they will adjust, and you can collect from a new expat. The Saudi House rental contract is also written in Arabic, so we have to sign it blindly. Even electricity bills are also issued in Arabic. We have to get help from my Arabic friends to read it initially.

In Bahrain that way it was similar to India. Contract is one page only in English on hundred fills stamp paper and rent we have to pay on monthly basis. For building caretaker will be there who takes care of maintenance of the house and collecting rent. Electricity bill also in English so we can read the amount and pay online. Now, Bahrain authorities have made it easier because electricity and water authority bill amounts will be deducted from bank accounts directly. There are three types of houses are available in the gulf. Fully furnished, semi furnished and unfurnished. For long term unfurnished or semi is good and for short term fully furnished is good to go. Compounded townships are more costlier but safe to stay with families. one of my friend purchased furniture and he had to sell it within 2 years due to pink slip by company and incurred heavy loss so after coming to Bahrain he opted for fully furnished.

There are many services we can pay online for driving license, car registration renewal, electricity bill payment, traffic contravention penalty payment etc.

Transportation

Initially transportation is a big problem as no civil transportation like India train, bus, metro, rikshaw are available. Taxis are available but costly. So, we have to take help from friends to take our family outside or drop and pick up from the airport.

Yanbu was not an international airport at that time in 2007 when I went there. Fortunately, I had a good room partner, S, who had purchased a car first after landing in KSA. I took his help to take my family from Jeddah airport to Yanbu. It is a long distance of 340 km, but we have to travel by car. Petrol was cheaper than water at that time in 2007. On the long 340 km, you have to fill up with petrol leaving the city; otherwise, on the road, there is no petrol station. You have to go inside the connecting village or get help from the traffic police who also give you petrol if tripped in between. If sand storm there it is difficult to drive on the road.

Hot and humid environment, Summer ban during July, August

In gulf, there are two seasons winter and summer. Rainy season is very small and missing almost. Temperatures goes up to 45 to 50 degrees C, but the humidity is very high, at about 80%. So, a combination of these makes unbearable conditions for human beings working in the open sun. All clothes become wet, and within one hour, all water comes out of the body. Yes, this is a really big change when we arrive in the gulf. Humidity is the main killer factor in the gulf. In July and August, there is a summer ban, and schools remain closed due to high temperature and humidity. The heat index (body feeling temperature) is the temperature combined with the humidity factor. Above the 55 heat Index, all direct work under the sun is stopped, and orange flags are placed at many locations for indication in industry.

For example, this morning, 19-8-2024, the temperature was 36 degrees centigrade, the humidity was 72 per cent, and the heat index was 57%, so as it is above 55-mark, work will be stopped in direct sun. During the daytime, the peak heat index went above 60. Yesterday also stopped, and now the real humidity month has started. July and August are the main months when humidity remains high, and if you go out, you will be completely wet, and clothes need to be changed. We have to keep a spare pair of clothes. Sometimes, accidents happen where children are locked in the school bus, as driver goes out of the bus without checking, and the child dies in the bus due to the hot temperature of the day.

Generally, I do some gardening work on Friday, like digging a pit for a new plant or changing the location of plants in the morning after taking warm water with lime. Recently, in August, I also became dehydrated due to working in the garden on Friday at my residence at 9 am. I started feeling uneasy, so I sat on the chair near the entrance of my home, but from the chair, I fell down and had a small head injury as it was raised place with three steps. First, my wife got confused about what to do. For time being I lost control and could not remember what happened. Then she rushed to our neighbour, and he came and helped me to get up and sit on the chair. Immediately, my friends were called by my wife, and they took me to the hospital. In the hospital, I had to take a wheelchair as I could not walk. In the hospital, doctor gave me a saline bottle in the vein, and within one hour, I started walking again.

During the June 2024 Hajj pilgrimage about 1300 pilgrims

died due to hot weather in KSA. Temperature went about 50 degrees Celsius at Makkah.

Language problem

Yes, language is a big problem initially, and that is also true if you are surrounded by local employees. For example, my friend D was an operator, and he was put in the control room. He was surrounded by local operators, so initially, he was not able to understand a single Arabic word. Yes, now, after six months, he has started speaking and understanding some words. So, there are benefits also. I heard Malayali people who run grocery stores in the Gulf learn Arabic very easily due to their contact with local people. My flat partner at Yanbu S was also living in a Lebanese labour camp, so he learned Arabic, which is now an advantage for him. My friend P also spent some time in Lebanon and he knows spoken Arabic.

Religion and culture shock:

Main religion in the gulf is Islam. If you have some knowledge of Islam it will help understand local festivals and some rules we need to follow during Ramadan. For example, in India we can drink water in the open during Ramadan but, if you drink in gulf it is an offence. One of my friends told me that his manager got deported from Saudi Arabia because of this mistake.

In Saudi, generally, two major holidays are Eid AL Fitr after Ramadan and Eid AL Adha and National Day leave. In Bahrain, 15 days public holidays we are getting annually. In addition to 2 Eid vacation we are getting Ashura holidays for 2 days 1 day each for New Year holiday for English as well as hijra new year, 2 days for national day, 1 day on labour day and 1-day Prophet's birthday. Also advantage in gulf is leave are counted for working days only so if I have 10 days leave, I can take 16 days vacation as Friday Saturday are not counted.

In India we go to our boss' house with family or our boss also comes to our house with family for a party or dinner. In gulf local people generally don't mix with expats so going to each other's house is not possible. Generally, they have their own family group within which they go to each other's house. Even companies sponsor Ramadan dinners at five-star hotels but it is only for male singles.

When I attended the first shutdown lunch party at Yanbu, I was shocked that no individuals were allowed to take lunch in separate dishes like buffet. All have to sit around a big dish about 1-meter diameter and eat like the Arabic way from a common big dish which was full of biryani and mutton pieces put on the top. Some sweet luqaimat and of course coke tins. I thought I would seat with Indian friends, but nobody was as they all were vegetarian. Finally, I asked permission from western employees of an American company with whom company had a 50:50 joint venture to sit with them. And they allowed me to join them.

One of my friends brought his father and mother to Saudi Arabia. I asked what the program is for sightseeing. I thought he would take them to Jeddah, which is the gateway to Hajj pilgrims and a metro city. He said, "In Saudi, I want to take them to see Makkah and Madinah." He did not know that non-Muslims cannot visit Makkah and Madinah. Now I saw an Indian women minister who recently visited Madinah, so they allowed her to visit Madinah. Generally, from Yanbu, our friends go to Jeddah, take family-furnished apartment, and stay there for two-three days, and come back.

Jeddah is somewhat cosmopolitan city and liberal as from all corners of the world people come for hajj so Jeddah was a gate way for them for hajj. The gold market is very big in Jeddah. I also went with family once and with friends another time. Visit was very enjoyable as there are many malls. Tall water fountain also there which is visible from distance. Which is known as king Fahd's fountain having 312 meter hight.

Rules and regulations

Rules in the gulf are very strict, and judgement is given immediately and there are no many layers of courts like India. In Saudi Arabia sharia law is followed. Also, not like India, it takes years to get judgment here in gulf judgement is very fast. So, it is better not to get involved in any legal problems. One of my friends did not purchase a car. When I asked why, he said in his company, one driver had killed one local in a road accident. He was in jail, and when he went to meet him, the driver was crying, saying they would behead him as in the Gulf if somebody dies in an accident, then the driver will be punished with the death penalty. Fortunately, the driver was released as his company convinced the family of the deceased person and convinced them to take some compensation money (blood money) and forgive this poor driver because his family would suffer if he was given the death penalty. Their family accepted blood money and granted him a pardon.

If family don't pardon there is no other way. Carrying drug also a punishable offence and punishment is death. Many expats get jail due to violation like traffic, theft, money irregularities, and illegal stay without proper work visa. At airport many times we see expats with police being deported due to illegal stay. In Riffa my car washing men was Bangladeshi one day he was caught by police and got deported.

Working hours

Working hours in government companies are 40 hrs. 8 hours per day for 5 days per week and for private companies 48 hours for 6 days per week. During Ramadan for Muslim employees working hours are 6 hours per day and for non-Muslim 8 hours per day.

Medical problem

Medical treatment is costly in the gulf compared to India. Medicine comes from European countries so medicine is also costly. If company isn't paying medical for family, it is difficult some time to bear family medical cost. Now my company has started family medical through insurance cards.

One of my young operator friends had pain in his left hand. He wanted to go to India for treatment, but he delayed it as his family was arrived at Bahrain for vacation. One day in the morning, he had a stroke, and went in to comma. He was under treatment in a government hospital in Manama for almost one month, and then he was sent back to India by a plane with a modified seat arrangement. Now, he has recovered, but not fully. You should be medically fit to serve in the gulf.

Police Case

After coming to the gulf, it is better to have no crime report. Some expat is involved in wrongdoing and when they are deported, they spoil the name of the country along with them. One expat was involved in a theft from the mall. He was deported after one month in jail.

Many expats take out loans from banks and purchase cars. If he loses his job, he will not be able to pay loan instalment. Bank will declare him a defaulter. In this case he cannot leave the country.

Traffic rule violations are also what many expats do and suffer penalties and jail.

Drug selling is punishable by death in Saudi Arabia. That is why if anybody give sealed cover in India to send it to Saudi friend or relatives don't accept, it should be in open condition so you are aware of the content. Liquid or semi liquid to carry in hand bag is not allowed like ghee, chyavanprash, jam. Chili powder, pickle powder etc. Swiss knife not allowed in handbag. I had lost chyavan prash and pickle masala as I carried in hand bag by mistake.

Chapter

10

Dos and Don't

Dos –

Working etiquettes

Working hard and sincerely will repay in any other form, so never get disheartened by boss behaviour or company policies. If you work hard and get bad results, try for an alternative job, but don't be less interested in the present job. Some expat leaves companies with bad names or bad acts like deleting soft files on the computer. And leaving job without proper handover. This will make a bad impression on the company and if you contact them to come back as a new job not suitable, they will not accept you.

As rightly said by Infosys CEO Narayan Moorthy that "Don't love your company but love your work because you don't know when your company stops loving you." On the last day of my working at Al Jubail company my boss asked me to finalize one repeat order with one contractor which we completed in last shutdown. I said I will do it till last hour of my working day. we finalized it and boss was happy.

Follow local rules and regulations.

Local rules by knowing or unknowingly should not be broken as "don't know" argument is not accepted by any court. Ramadan rules should be studied before landing, poppy seed is ban in gulf and religious hatred not tolerated in the gulf so keep note of it. In some gulf countries like Saudi and Kuwait drinking alcohol is not allowed. In Dubai and Bahrain, it is freely allowed.

Respect local religion and culture

When you live in another country there may be different religions, rituals and culture. Try to respect that religion, culture and rituals. Now we all should understand that we all have plus and minus points and the best thing is to accept the best from others and continue our journey of getting continuous improvement. Do appreciate Arabic food which you liked as it is less spicy and less chilli but more nutritious. Grilled non veg are really healthy as in India we add more oil in non veg and make it more heavy food.

Follow the rules during Ramadan

During Ramadan certain rules should be followed so try to learn about that. You cannot consume food or water in public during day time. Carrying water and food in transparent bag is not allowed. Nowadays there are many videos available which teaches how to follow the Ramadan rules. Restaurants and canteens remain closed day time during Ramadan. Bar and wine shops also remains closed during Ramadan in Bahrain.

Follow company rules

Company rules and procedures are very important, so a violation of it may lead to the termination of the job. During Covid, many employees lost their jobs due to small minor mistakes like coming to duty with Covid symptoms and coming to the hospital without a test. Which were taken very seriously and they were terminated.

Don'ts –

Don't involve in political and religious discussion

Some people have a habit of discussing everything from politics to economics to religion and posting on social media. If, in the Gulf, you discuss the politics of India, it is ok, but the local political or religious discussion better to avoid. One teacher got deported because she asked student to say morning greeting by one religious god name..

Most of gulf countries are respecting all the religions and allows them to practice as per individual faith. But if you feel superior and try to criticize local religions of the region, it may be viewed seriously and may result in serious consequences like jail and deportation.

Similarly, there are conflicts between some countries and if you take the side of one country on social media which is not liked by local countrymen and if any one complain you will be out from that country.

Don't quarrel

Don't get involved in quarrelling with others, fighting also brings company action or police action and finally deporting.

At Yanbu, one of my friends called one night and said that I should help him find some room for him as he had a quarrel with his roommate. He was from Mumbai and was staying with one friend from Kerala on a room-sharing basis. The quarrel was about cleaning the kitchen platform after cooking. I told him I am at present staying with my family in a furnished apartment as my family came from India for a visit. So, if you want, go to my room and stay for a while. He went there and stayed with my friend S. Second day in canteen he said sir don't pay for lunch I will pay for your lunch as you helped me. I told him that I helped him as an Indian I have to help you and no need to pay for my lunch. He even asked permission from his company to lodge a police complaint against his roommate. But his company did not allow him. When he went to India on vacation, he received mail from his company that your service was no longer required, so he could not come back from vacation, and his chapter was closed.

Don't do traffic violations.

In the Gulf, traffic violations have high penalties. Sometimes, they are also sent to jail. One of our colleagues met with an accident and he crossed the red light and hit another vehicle and got jail terms for a few days. After his arrival, he had to present at the department safety meeting and narrate his incident in his department as a lesson learned for others so other employees wouldn't do it again.

Don't carry following

Don't carry wine, pork, drug, poppy seeds and porn films to Saudi Arabia as they are prohibited.

Chapter

11

Important Documents

Passport: Passport of self-spouse and children are important document and always should be carried in separate bag carefully. In Saudi, passports are held by a sponsor company and given back to the expats only when he is going on officially approved vacation. In other countries passport remains with expat only. Sometime passport validity expires and employee remains in home country so it will create problem. Always see that for passport minimum six-month validity there before going on vacation. It is better to renew passport in gulf country only as it is easy and convenient. Local Indian embassy or authorised agent process renewal faster than Indian passport office and also easy to get Bahrain visa on new passport number.

One of my friends lost his wife's passport at Yanbu airport and went to Jeddah for dropping her at air port to go back to India. At Jeddah when immigration officer asked about passport she could not find. They had to come back from Jeddah and searched for passport at Yanbu airport, fortunately they got it from Yanbu airport security.

Visa: Work visa for self and dependent resident visa for spouse and children. Also periodically check visa status is valid on LMRA web site. Earlier they used to paste sticker in passport but now separate papers are issued which we have to carry or carry soft copy in mobile. Earlier visa sticker were pasted on passport pages but, now visa are provided on separate papers which is saving passport papers.

Ticket: Air ticket for all family members. Credit card thru which ticket are booked should be with expats. If he has booked using friends credit card it is advisable to keep photo copy deleting CVV no. when family member travelling alone without credit card thru which it is booked. Family must carry photo copy of credit card. One time I had booked ticket using my friends credit card and forgot to carry his credit cards photocopy. I was questioned by airline employee at Mumbai. He said you cannot travel, I said ok I will pay for it please give me refund after I reach destination. Now he was confused how to refund. He told his boss and his boss after seeing me released from paying in cash.

Appointment letter: Generally, first time going employee carries with him a file prepared by an agent which contains appointment order, visa, ticket etc. If no file is given by agents all document containing file should be prepared by expat and kept in hand bag so that he can show it to immigration officer.

Degree certificate: Degree certificate will be required again to present at joining company in the gulf. They will require it to submit it to get engineers license form local government authority.

Marriage certificate: A marriage certificate will be required to get a Saudi iqama or Bahrain's CPR ID card. Also, for getting visa from UK or USA it needs to be carried to show it to visa officer. Generally Indian embassy issues it at respective gulf country based on Indian passports.

Medical certificate: A medical certificate will be required to present upon joining the company. They will again get all medical tests done at local hospitals approved by the government.

Birth certificate of children: Birth certificate of children will be required to get a visa and local ID card. To get school admission also it will be required.

School leaving certificate: For school admission of children, a school leaving certificate will be required.

NRI certificate: After landing in gulf countries NRI certificates are issued by the Indian embassy of the concerned gulf country. This is required at some point if any notice related to income tax or NRI status issued from the income tax in India.

CPR/ Iqama: These are local ID cards that are required to be present when asked by local police or authorities. It is also required for opening a bank account, money transfer and a driver's license. At the bank, they will not ask for a bank account number or name but will ask for CPR No. in Bahrain

Driving license: Driving license is very important as in gulf there is little public transport developed. Getting a driving license also takes 6 months to 1 year as there are two types of test. One is a computer test and the second is a practical driving test. I passed the computer test in one go at Al Jubail but failed in the practical test. After three attempt I passed practical test. In Dubai UAE driving license is more difficult to get and costly too.

Credit cards: For payment of any charges like extra baggage charges above allowable we have to pay at the airport. So better to carry credit cards. Also, for purchasing some food items like coffee or tea or breakfast you need to pay so either carry cash or credit card.

In Saudi, it happened that my wife was going back to India with another friend's wife. At Dammam airport the flight was cancelled after immigration so the airline arranged hotel accommodation in a five-star hotel. In the hotel food was free but water was chargeable. So, my wife had some money in cash so she paid from her pocket but my friend's wife did neither carry money nor a mobile phone. So, my wife helped her.

Chapter

12

Myths and Exceptions

There are some myths about the gulf in India, which needs to be clarified before coming to the gulf.

1. **There will be a shortage of water as there will be no rain, so there are no lakes and rivers.**

This is the biggest but logical myth. But after staying in the gulf, I can say that this is not true. Water is available in ample amounts because of science and seawater. From seawater, steam is produced by heating water, power is generated by turbine, from steam turbine exhaust low pressure steam is condensed, which is used as drinking water. So, power is a by-product, and sweet water is the main product of power plants in the Gulf. Very big power stations and sweet water plants are there in the gulf. And natural gas is used to heat the water in boilers. Natural gas is amply available in Gulf countries due to the biggest producers of oil and gas in the world, so, water will be there till oil and gas reserve last. It is true that there is no river in the gulf. Saudi Arabia has large empty land in south side called Rub Al khali on which they can construct solar power station. it is the world largest sand sea.

2. **In Muslim countries, there may be strict rules, and women will have more restrictions.**

Yes, this was true some years ago for Saudi Arabia, but now Saudi also bringing new rules every day and has changed a lot. The new regime wants to make the Saudi like a European tourist-friendly country from a strict religious country, and has changed Saudi Arabia by taking drastic actions. NEOM smart city project is very unique and when it will be completed in 2039, it will be wonder on the earth.

When I was in Saudi from 2007 to 2010 all women had to wear abaya, they cannot travel alone, they cannot drive cars.

New regime has taken over many drastic changes have taken place. Now women are given car driving license expat women's can wear clothes of their choice but proper dress. And many new job openings are there for women. Still many more to be done to be at par with European countries.

When I went to Saudi in 2007 there were very strict rules and I had to purchase an abaya for my wife and daughter from India before going. My daughter was feeling very uncomfortable and asked me why women are not free for clothes to wear of their own choice? I had to convince her that here it is rules of this country and as an expat we have to obey.

3. **Vegetables and fruits will not be available easily as it is a desert in the gulf,**

Vegetables and fruits are coming from all around the world. So we get mango all the seasons and some known variety of vegetables all the time like cabbage, big potatoes, cauliflowers, spinach, tomatoes, brinjals big, brinjal long, brinjal small mushrooms, zucchini etc., Yes we miss Indian vegetables like Guar sing(cluster beans), Tandalja bhaji(Amaranth leaves), Tuvar sing(Pigeon peas), Surti papdi(broad bean seeds), Green garlic leaves, and Patra (Taro leaves) etc.

Some of the vegetables and fruits come from Saudi Arabia like potatoes, brinjal, watermelon etc. Hass avocado comes from Mexico which is better in taste than avocado from African countries. Avocado I could taste after coming to gulf. From Srilanka curry patta leaves and other vegetables are imported.

As majority Indians are from Kerala state in the gulf and Kerala businessmen run malls so, vegetables from Kerala are available all the time. Like jackfruit, banana, small banana kaskdali, pumpkin, coconut green and dry, coconut water, coconut milk, coconut powder, coconut oil, coconut grated, banana stem, banana flowers, banana leaves, yam, drumstick, drumstick leaves, kari patta etc. Many Kerala recipes we tested after coming to the gulf like appam, avial, erissery, idiyappam, rasam, payasam, medu vada, set dosa, Kerala sweets, etc.

Idli dosa which is now among the top world-famous breakfast. My Arabic friend also eats it and appreciates it. Avial is a very old recipe from Kerala and it was invented by Bhim of pandav of

Mahabharat during his stay at king Virat's residence. Bhim was serving as cook in king Virat's kitchen during hiding period. It is a mix of vegetables with curd and coconut.

Fruits like apples, oranges, lemons, mangoes, plum, lychee, grapes, avocado, watermelon and muskmelon, dates, kaka fruit, kiwi, rambutan, pineapple, pomelo, etc. come from India, Pakistan, Philippines, Europe, America Africa etc.

4.   Indian Food items may not be available easily in the gulf.

Now, Indians are everywhere, so their food is easily available in all corners of the world. Though vegetarian restaurants are very few, people from Gujarat may face difficulties, but now, many pure veg restaurants are also opening where vegetarian dishes are served. South Indian dishes like Idly dosa, sambar, appam, upma, idiyappam, etc. Punjabi items like kadi pakoda, paneer tikka, rajma chawal, etc. Nowadays, home delivery is more used by locals and expatriates to get food home delivered instead of restaurants. Delivery boy on scooter are seen throughout the night in Bahrain. Here it is Talabat like Zomato in India.

At Sharjah airport I tested another variety of dosa that is chicken tikka masala dosa. In Bahrain chilli idly and Manchurian idly fusion recipes are available in south Indian restaurants.

Kerala has their special dishes like sadhya dish, where rice, fish curry, chicken curry, sweet, chutney etc are served on banana leaves. Many types of chutney are their speciality. Bamboo biryani is a very special dish in which they cook chicken biryani in a bamboo cylinder and piston and serve it directly from bamboo. Chettinad restaurants, Udupi restaurants, madras cafe, sangita, gaurikrishna etc are seen in gulf.

Jackfruit biryani and jackfruit shake are special from kerala. In the gulf recipes from milk shake, fruit juice and avocado juice paysam, are also available. One of my western friends asked me what is rasam and idly? I replied it is hot tamarind soup and rice cake.

Local People eat less spicy food, but now locals also sometimes visit Indian restaurants for vegetarian food. Idly dosa is preferred by them as being a light and full meal.

Rice is consumed maximum in the gulf that is basmati rice which is used in cooking biryani. All leading brands of basmati rice from India, Pakistan are available easily and of the best quality. In Saudi I saw many types of rice like kabsa rice, sayadia rice, lemon rice, saffron rice, tom yum rice, tamarind rice.

Wheat flours are available from India. Before some time, export of wheat and wheat flour was banned by government of India so some Indian company opened flour mill in UAE and make flour from imported Australian wheat. Now Indian spices and food grain, ready to eat food and dairy products are available in all Indian malls like LULU, Mega mart, Nesto and AL Adil.

5.   Milk and milk products may be very costly in the Gulf

There is a very big dairy Almarai in Saudi Arabia which caters to milk, buttermilk (Laban), labneh, cheese, paneer, curd, sweet-flavoured curd, humus, etc. One of my friend takes.

Buttermilk, known as Laban, is available in the gulf. It is thick and is made from milk directly and sold at the same price as milk; in India, it is thin like water as butter is removed, and the remaining water is sold at a lower price than milk. But the taste of Laban is far better, and once you drink and use it, you will not like other thin buttermilk. Many types of Curd and flavoured curds, Laban and flavoured Laban and fruit juices are sold in the gulf. due to hot and humid weather condition fruit juices and laban drinks are more used in gulf. Some are very specific, like tamarind juice, blueberry juice, kiwi lemon juice etc.

Indian dairy products are also available in the gulf including shrikhand (waterless curd with sugar and cardamom), or saffron or mango cheese, paneer and butter, ghee, gulab jamun etc from Amul India in Indian malls.

Many well-known brands of dairy products come from Europe such as cheese, paneer, chocolates, and Greek yoghurt. Mozzarella cheese are widely used for pizza making. Parmesan cheese are used in other recipes. Arabic cheese is sour in taste and used with salad.

Chapter

13

Rolls Of Mentors In Life

The role of a mentor is very much important as without a mentor, we may make mistakes, and some mistakes can change our lives, which we cannot reverse them even if we know that they were wrong. So, to minimize mistakes, a mentor is very much required.

In life, we get mentoring from our parents, teachers, friends, brothers, sisters, and many others. For example, without my guru Manharbhai Sir, I would not have achieved Sangeet Visharad in Indian classical music in vocal (BA music Vocal). It was a very lengthy course of six years, but with his smiling face and tolerance, we passed six years like six months.

Also, in professional life my ex-boss Dushyant Chhaya, whom I cannot forget, always pushed us to do our jobs independently and make mistakes and learn. He pushed us to face higher management without any fear as he was always telling us we are behind you, please go and attend meetings with higher management. They are also human like us.

Another ex-boss was Mr. Ashok Joshipura who gave me full freedom to do the job and always worked with us like a friend and not a boss. We always felt free and discussed anything and everything with him without any hesitation. One day I met him in a bank in Vadodara when I went on vacation. But before some years he expired.

Similarly, writing books was my years old desire and ambition. but without proper direction and guidance it started and stopped many times. Consistency in writing was not there. What to write and what not, how to start, how many pages, audience should be focused to make it best seller and what will be structure, what is the easiest way to write a book etc. In date wise diary form or other form many questions were there and there was no direction. Fiction or non-fiction.

Then, I joined the book writing free boot camp course of Dr Kailash Pinjani on 6 and 7 July 2024. He explained step by step the book writing method and stages of book writing, common mistakes of writers, reader's perspective writing etc., which enlightened me, and I could complete my first book. I thank him and give full credit to him for my first book. Then I joined his paid course in which we learned many new things in the field of book writing like computer apps and software available to write books, voice typing and Grammarly are very amazing tools. Then I signed agreement with him for queen package and started my book journey.

Without his continuous guidance, and boosting my book-writing dream would not have been completed, and my dream of becoming an author would have been a dream forever.

Chapter

14

Books Which Inspired Me

In my child hood I stayed with my grandparents and effect of my grandparents was more in my life. I thank my grandfather Muljibhai, who, besides being a poor farmer from the small tribal village Vavdi in district Narmada, Gujarat India maintained one small library in a wooden scrap box of size around 1-metre cube. In Childhood, I read religious books like Geeta, Ramayana and Mahabharata, Amar Charitra and Okha Haran, which played a major role in my life. I liked many characters from Mahabharat but Yudhishthira and Krishna were main. Yudhishthira for his habit of speaking truth and Krishna for doing something new and breaking the old outdated rituals. First step to become writer is to become a good reader first. All religious stories book he had in library were completed by me. I used to be a very religious person in those days, and I fasted with him many Hindu pious days. In adhik mas (an extra month every 4 years in the Hindu Vikram Samvat calendar), I still remember how in the early morning, at 5 am, I with my grandfather and grandmother went walking 8 km from my village Vavdi to the nearby river Narmada at Rampura village and took a bath and temple visit and coming back by bus. My grandfather was known as a bhagat (priest), and he used to do some bhajans kirtans the whole night on full moon day (Poonam) at each street member's house. In the month of Shravan, he would read Mahabharat daily at night, with the help of kerosene lamp as electricity was not there in my village. Street members used to visit our house to hear him. He was a respectable leader in our street. Some priest also come to our house from Mehsana district and staying for month. They will do some astrology and puja prayer at customer home and collect food and money from them. At evening they will ask my grandmother to cook khichdi using half water and half butter oil from their earning in separate vessel. We just see this food as we cannot eat it and consider them how rich they are!

The last person I thank is my father, Doctor Lalit Chandra, who was an MBBS doctor and was a strong follower of Dr Ambedkar and Lord Buddha and gave me a logical and scientific way of thinking and delinked me from religious thoughts and blind faiths and led a scientific way of life. My father was a clever student and went to Ahmedabad to be admitted to a science college with 20 rupees in hand. Somehow, he got admission to a government hostel and became the first MBBS doctor in my birthplace village, Vavdi district, Narmada, Gujarat.

He served for five years in the government primary health centre in Hansot, PHC. Then, he opened his private clinic at

Hansot and served there for about 20 years. Unlike other doctors who always preferred cities, he liked rural life and wished to open a clinic in a village which should be pollution free and on the bank of a river. Hansot was fulfilling all his three requirements as it was a small-village place with no major industry except cotton gin and on the banks of one of the tributaries of river Narmada, which was visible from our house. He was serving 24 by 7, and whenever any patient came, he never said no. Sometimes, in the monsoon season whole night, farmers used to bring patients in bullock carts to our dispensary. It is a very noble profession, and at that time, respect for doctors was very high in society.

When he died in a road accident in 1996, I still remember in a condolence meeting, one poor farmer came and told the gathering that he prayed to God that again late doctor get birth in Hansot and become a doctor again. It made our eyes full of tears. My father's ambition was to become president of India. He joined one political party Janata party also during emergency in 1975. He was vice president in local school management committee. In another incident told by one school principal was also unforgettable. He was leader of congress party and my father was in janta party so both were rival of each other and had wide differences on various subject. One day his daughter got pain due to pregnancy and no other doctors were available in the village. He sent his wife to call him considering if he goes my father will not come. My father told me to accompany him and when we reached their home, principal just became emotional and told, doctor I thought you will not come for visit as we are from opposite party. My father replied I came as a doctor and we take oath to serve anybody who call us so, I came for my duty as a doctor and not as a political leader! Principal narrated this incident in condolence meeting and said he was noble personality.

The story of Buddha and his disciple Purna was very inspiring which we studied from our school books. When Purna wanted to go to the next village for preaching and he was asking permission, Buddha asked him some questions. Purna, if they will abuse you, what will you do? Purna replied I would think that they are abusing only and not beating me. Buddha again asked him, but if they beat you, then? Purna replied I will think they are beating only but not killing me. But if they kill, then? Then I will think if I get death in return for preaching that, this is the best death I will get. In any case, I have to die one day. So why not to die for a good cause? Buddha said Purna, you have passed the exam. Now, nobody can stop you. Go ahead.

This story reminds me that prepare for worst conditions than present, then you will be able to sustain in present condition. Budhdha's preaching always inspired and guided me in the time of confusion.

One of my bosses was very rude and used to fire employees, mainly Indian, at the rate of 2 employees per month. I told his near-favourite employee that we have to prepare ourselves mentally for going back home if we get fired. What maximum he can do harm for us? Once we are ready for being fired, we will have no fear of him and will have the courage to stand in front of him. He said he liked my reply.

The first book I read was the Gujarati translation "'Jindagi jitvani jadibutti" from the English book "How to Win Friends and Influence People" by Dale Carnegie.

He teaches us how to behave and how to turn people and friends in our favour from negative to positive. How do you become zero enemy status by filtering your language? With so many examples and live demos, he explained that you could become a public figure and turn situations in your favour. Very nice book and the best seller in the world. I learnt many things from it.

The best lessons learnt from this book is "you can make more friends in two months by becoming interested in other people than you can in two years by trying to get other people interested in you."

The second book which inspired me is in my mother tongue language, Gujarati, written by Nanji Kalidas Mehta. His book name is "Sapna Sagar Paarna", which means "Overseas Dreams," which is the autobiography of Mr Nanji

Kalidas Mehta, an Indian businessman in Uganda. He was 4th standard pass and went as a helper in grocery shops in Uganda from Porbandar Gujarat, India. After serving in the shop, he expressed his wish to open a new shop in a nearby village, which was supported by his shop owner, and he started the new shop. Their main business was import-export of food items and spices, which means he was importing things that were not produced in Uganda and exporting those that were produced in Uganda. From the shop, his growth story started, and then he started sugar mills and then cotton mills, and so on. Once upon a time, he became the leading industrialist of Uganda, and the Ugandan government was sending him as their official representative in Western countries. Also, so many Gujarati businessmen were present in Uganda, that on currency notes one of the languages in which currency was mentioned was Gujarati language.

During President Idi Amin's time, he expelled all foreigners, including Indians, from Uganda with very short notice and without any money. He thought foreigners were taking away the profit, and that is why his countrymen were poor. The people who were expelled from Uganda went to UNO's Human Rehabilitation Commission and requested them for proper rehabilitation. UNO distributed affected 100 families to each developed country and asked them to provide citizenship and jobs. So that way, all Indians, mainly

Gujarati, became worldwide entities. So, sometimes, it is said to be a blessing in disguise. Now, the new government of Uganda wants those businessmen back, but nobody wants to go back. Because all sugar mills were closed due to mismanagement after expat left Uganda. Once a sugar exporting country Uganda became sugar importing country.

From Nanji Kalidas Mehta I learned that if 4th standard pass men can go abroad and become the top most industrialists of Uganda, I am a mechanical engineer with 20 plus years' experience in the oil and gas field, the most demanded field in the gulf. Why can't I do it, if he can?

He narrated in his book how the atmosphere was hostile and malaria-prone and how he used to travel in Uganda by a carriage lifted by four men. He gave very generous donations to Gandhiji, the father of the nation of India, and also opened a school and hostel for girls in Porbandar, Gujarat, India. He narrated how a maneater gang was killing Indians and others and eating them in Victoria Lake. At that time all African and Asian countries where it was British rule, citizens from one country to another country could migrate very easily as no visa required. So, the Gujarati business community, like goldsmith (soni) bohra Muslim, patels migrated to many British-ruled countries and settled there. Some days back, I met some workers who came in my company from Uganda in Bahrain. I asked who is the top industrialists in Uganda, and he gave us two Indian Guajarati industrialist names.

Madhwani and Ruparelia.

After coming to Bahrain, I learned that the first community that came from India to Bahrain was the goldsmith Thattai Bhatia community from Gujarat, who built a 200-year-old Krishna temple in the heart of central Manama. They have many gold shops in Manama and east Riffa. Some have become citizens of Bahrain, too. Now, no doubt, Malayali people are the main expat Indian population in Bahrain. Because after coming from Gujarat, goldsmith people did not venture into other areas, businesses like malls, grocery shops, education, schools, medical hospitals, etc. Kerala Malayali people occupied all these fields, and now they are number one in the Gulf. Many times, we call it Malayalam, which is the number two language after the local language, Arabic. In Bahrain, Hindi and Malayalam songs are also played on the radio. We used to hear Malayalam songs as they were based on classical music and were sweet. Now, at present Hindi songs are not hindi songs but punjabi songs, and there is no Hindi words or classical music in them.

In the industry, notice boards in Hindi, English, and Arabic are the main languages of the workforce. Even red buses of local transport, boards are placed in Hindi in Bahrain.

Similarly, almost all countries have an Indian population, whether it is the UK, USA, or Australia, you name it. One of my Bahraini friends told me Indians are like oxygen; they are everywhere. We were working in the same department and seating for two years in one office. I learned many Arabic words from him. Like khalas, salam alaikum, shabba khair, sakh barak, slonek, zain etc. He told me he had visited India's Taj Mahal and Vadodara, my native place. In Agra, many people could not distinguish him as a foreigner. In Bahrain, I saw many locals who looked like Indian.

Many times, I discussed with him which habits of Indian he didn't like. He said keeping too much distance between cars at the traffic signal, driving at low speed in the high-speed lane and tobacco chewing and spitting on the road at the signal by opening the driver-side window. He sometimes visited Indian restaurants to eat vegetarian food like idly dosa, but he didn't like that the cleaning person and serving person were the same, so he was doubtful regarding whether he washed his hands or not after cleaning the table.

The Bohra Muslim community from Gujarat also migrated from Gujarat and settled in many African and gulf countries. They are businessmen primarily and have very unique cap and coloured abaya from which one can recognize them very easily. Very polite and soft-spoken people.

The Pakistani people also migrated in large numbers to England, and now they have a mayor of Pakistan origin in London. In the same way, from Indian origin, Rishi Sunak also became prime minister of the UK recently. Many MPs of

Indian origin are in the UK parliament. My ex-boss in Saudi Arabia's parents also migrated from Gujarat to Karachi, Pakistan during partisan, and then he migrated to the USA. After getting a degree from the USA, he came to the Gulf as a project manager in one of the petrochemical companies.

My formula of success is equal to 50 per cent intelligence plus 50 per cent daring. If you are 100% intelligent but have 0% daring you cannot take decisions. For example, if mahatma Gandhi would have stayed and studied in India only, he would have not become great leader so, bad or good you have to make decisions. He studied in UK and practiced law in south Africa that made him global leader.

Swami Sachchidananda's books "Adhogati nu mul varna vyavstha" and "Bharat na yudhdho no itihas" also inspired me a lot. He has discovered why India remained slave for 1000 years, due to Varnavyavstha. It is a hierarchical unequal society based on work having unequal distribution of wealth and respect. From four varnas there are thousands of castes and caste is class in India. The people of India suffered a lot due to the upper middle and lower caste division of society. People were divided into 4 varnas according to livelihood. Brahmin had the right to education. Kshatriya had the right to rule and fight the war, Vaishya had the right to business, and Shudras had the right to serve. Of 4 varna of people, only Kshatriya had the right to fight with enemies. So, only 25 % of people had the right to fight; others had to surrender only. At the same time, nearby Afghanistan had complete warrior people. So, whenever they need wealth and slaves they announce, who wants to come to India for an attack? Many soldiers came together and attacked India, mainly temples, looting gold, silver, and slaves and then distributing among them according to their numbers of soldiers. Mahmud Gazni invaded India 17 times and looted Somnath temple.

In "Bharat na yudhdho no Itihaas" history of Indian wars book swami narrated what common mistakes were done by Indian kings during war with enemies and how enemies were able to gain victory even with less manpower. How India was divided in small princely states and they used to make war between them instead of uniting and fighting against invaders from Afghanistan and Iran.

Swami says those who migrate are the richest in the world. See any background of any community who migrated. For example, Patel migrated from Punjab to Gujarat and Parsi migrated from Iran, Marwaris migrated from Rajasthan and kachchhi Gujarati migrated from Gujarat To Mumbai and they are the richest community in Mumbai. In present Patel and Shahs migrated to the USA are the richest community in the USA among Indians. Motels and Patels have become synonyms in US. One Patel has written book "Kadi to Kansas " in which he narrated how he could brought Patel's from his village of India to USA.

Similarly, there was plague spread in the village of Karnataka and people were dying on a daily basis. So old people advised young people to leave the village and migrate to some safer place. So, Shetty youth from Karnataka migrated and started idly dosa street shops in Mumbai and now become millionaires and owners of 5-star hotels. One dosa king restaurant was there in Manama which was making more than 100 varieties of dosa. Its owners success story was also very inspiring.

Another book which impressed me is PMBOK. During PMP course I studied, PMBOK and other books related to project management. It helped me a lot in professional as well as personal life. There are many important rules in project management.

What is a project? as per PMI project is a temporary endeavour undertaken to create a unique product, service or result. Project has a start date, finish date and uniqueness. As such we human beings are also a project on this earth because we have birth date, death date and uniqueness. No human beings are identical.

There are many topics in project management, such as integration management, scope management, cost management, time management, quality management, HR management, communication management, risk management, procurement management, stakeholder management. All these are important in our day-to-day life because we have to manage a project for example daughters or sons' marriage or building new house. All these chapters are involved in it, and if we know how to handle all these aspects, a marriage or home making project will be completed within time and cost.

"Risk is everywhere". So, you can manage the risk but, cannot avoid the risk. Risk has to be mitigated in a systematic manner by keeping a risk register and what the risk is and how to mitigate it. In every meeting of project management risk needs to be discussed. Every time new risk emerges and it has positive or negative impact on project. Covid was new risk which we never encountered before and many projects got delayed due to it.

Project managers spend ninety per cent of their time in communication.

Conflict is inevitable.

80/20 rule: 80% of problems are due to 20% root causes.

According to Tuckman Jensen, the newly formed team went through five stages of development.

Forming

Storming

Norming

Performing

Adjourning

In our normal life we also experience these five stages when we join a job in a new company or a newly married bride arrives at her husband's house. So, during the forming and storming stage if we keep patience, and undermine small mistakes in further stage norming and performing, there will be success. Many marriages break up during the storming stage only.

Chapter

15

Lonely Life In Gulf

Staying alone in the Gulf is very difficult and requires a strong willpower and stamina. Many expats cannot withstand this single life condition, which leads to a stressful life, gloomy life, alcoholic life, spending money in bars and dance bars, and some commit suicide also. Some go back to India. Many expats, mostly workers in the Gulf, are living lonely in the labour camp. There are many reasons for a lonely life. Like following.

1.   Single status visa

2.   Family status but children studying in India, so spouse cannot come

3.   Spouse is working in India, so cannot live together

4.   Parents are aged

Single-status visas are given to many non-technical and technical worker jobs. They cannot bring their family because the company doesn't want to take the burden of tickets and medical and education for the family. Some countries also discourage bringing families to the Gulf, so unskilled workers cannot bring their families to the Gulf. Saudi Arabia has recently imposed a

400 SAR per person per month visa charge for dependents, so many expats have sent their families back to India because this is uneconomical for them.

Some expats have grown-up children and are studying in India, so they don't want to disturb their studies. Also, some places in gulf don't have Indian schools run by Indian embassy so they cannot afford American school fees or British school fees and it is not reimbursed by company so they are also compelled to keep family in India.

Also, if children are above 18 years old, they cannot stay in Gulf countries unless they have college admission and are staying with their family on student visas. Now, there is a golden visa scheme in Bahrain, so if an expat has a minimum 2000 BHD basic salary per month and stays in Bahrain for more than 5 years, he is eligible for a golden visa for 10 years. He has to apply online for his and his family to pay the required fees of 300 BD per person and get the golden visa. He can call his children as they also get golden visas. So, expats who have children in India and want to bring them frequently apply for golden visa. Many of my friend have applied for golden visa and got it in one day.

Some expats have a working wife in India and don't want to resign and bring family in gulf so they also don't bring family except for some months during holidays. If the wife is an employee of the government department or companies, she will not like to leave that company. If their wife is working in India, it serves double benefit as there is no guarantee how many years an expat will stay in gulf country, so if in home country spouse is working then it serves as a factor of safety or plan B for risk mitigation for the risk of job loss in the terms of project management.

When I came to gulf my children were grown up and studying in college and school so, I could not bring my family to gulf. My wife was working in a semi government company so, she could not resign and come to the gulf and live a housewife life.

Some expat has aged and medically unfit father and mother so to take care of them he cannot bring family to the gulf. Also, sometimes, a single parent living in India so he cannot bring a family. Recently, one of my friend's instrument engineer from my current company moved to India to take care of his aged parents and joined an MNC in Bangalore. Another friend sent his family to India as his father died due to a heart attack and nobody to take care of mother. One of my friends went back to India to support his children's education as his working wife could not cope up. Now, he wants to come back to the gulf as his children are settled, but now, after 50, it is rare to get a job.

How to pass the time and how to manage a lonely life is a big question in the Gulf. In government companies, there are five days a week. So, Friday and Saturday are holidays. Friday is easy to pass as washing, cleaning and shopping are generally done on weekends. But another day, Saturday is difficult to pass. I used to walk in the morning and evening with my walking partner friend. Also made another friend as a picture partner. Every weekend we go to a cinema to watch Indian movies. Also, I have a degree in Indian classical music, so I used to record some of my favourite songs after doing rigorous practice and rehearsals and upload them on YouTube. As time passed, you set up in lonely life, but even though cooking every day and cleaning every day forced us to take lunch or dinner outside.

Walking is enjoyable in winter in the gulf but punishment in summer. In summer, humidity goes as high as 90 per cent, so if you go for a walk outside, you have to change all your clothes and wear new clothes. The temperature has been rising since morning. Even the 8 am temperature is unbearable due to the combination with humidity. July and August remain the hottest days, and generally, a summer ban applies during these months. The school remains closed, and work in open sunlight is prohibited from 12 to 4 pm. Many times, incidents have occurred that people die due to heat stroke.

During summer days daily temperature and humidity are closely monitored in company and if heat index goes beyond 55 work is stopped in open. It is insisted to carry water bottle always when going for site visit in industry. One day I had a site visit and the contractor team lead asked who came with the water bottle. I showed mine and he was happy, he also arranged water bottles from the contractor's side.

If you don't have any hobbies like cooking, singing or gardening, walking, sports etc. it is difficult to survive in the gulf alone. So, first start cooking at home and learn all basic things like tea, snacks like omelette upma, poha, bhajiya, shira, chapati, rice, dal, vegetables curry etc. still I don't know chapati properly. Uneven shape roti chapati I can make but the exact round shape is difficult for me. One of my friend put all the recipe paper on display in kitchen as he was learning cooking. even how to cut vegetable also on display.

Now there are ample Indian restaurants so we can order but still if you want light, hygienic, less spicy food you have to learn cooking otherwise you have to learn living on noodles, pizza and pasta and khabush.

In India, we were a working couple, and my time of home coming was earlier than my wife's, so some items like dal or sabji I used to make and roti chapati my wife will make. I thank chef Sanjeev Kapoor for his serial Khana Khazana, through which I learnt a lot of items. Later, it became a hobby for me. I wrote one full notebook from his episodes and tried all the good recipes like idly, dosa, sambhar, chicken biryani, etc.

I had a movie friend so we used to drive and see movies in nearby malls. We had one MNC bank credit card through which if you book a ticket with this card, you get a 50 percent discount. In gulf theatres even if you are one or two persons, movies will start as per schedule. It happened that we were only two people and saw a movie as if it was special premier show arranged for us.

Other good destinations were the city centre and the European Furniture Mall and other malls, where we used to go for walks. The city Centre of Bahrain is the largest mall, and all international brands of clothes are available there; it is somewhat costly but quality items are sold there. It is mainly the Saudi people's first choice of shopping. We generally avoid going there on holiday Friday or Saturday, as there are so many rushes from Saudi. On other days, it is easy to park a car, but on holidays, it's more difficult. They have made a 5-story building adjacent to the city Centre for car parking. But sometimes it is difficult to get parking. Also going in and coming out of the parking building takes one hour due to long queues of cars.

Lonely life and sickness are deadly combination which demotivates expats mentally and sometimes thinks of going back. You have to be healthy for living lonely life in the gulf. Food control and exercise makes body fit and yoga and meditation makes mind strong we have to remember that no pain no gain. Many lonely expats cry when they hear Pankaj Udhas song Chiththi aayi hey aayi hey chiththi aayi hey bade dino ke baad hum de vachno ko yaad vatan ki mitti aayi hey ... means letter has come from my mother land after long time and we remind commitments and it is like soil from my mother land has arrived.

When my younger brother Mrugesh arrived in Bahrain for 4 years deputation I felt happy as I was staying alone that time. His Bank transferred him for 4 years deputation at Bahrain branch.

In case of emergency I can call him. In foreign land if you have relatives its like blessing.

Kerala people have complete family staying in gulf so they feel more homely in gulf. The biggest building in Bahrain among Indians is of Kerala Samajam.

Chapter

16

My Covid Experience

During Covid, I went to India twice, and both times, I became Covid positive. It came like a big challenge to mankind, and the first wave was very panicked. Many people lost their jobs. Whether to go to the office or not, that was also a question mark. Masks and hand washing became compulsory. Still my hands are dry due to excessive use of hand sanitizer liquid. I have to apply Vaseline daily on my hand. There was a periodical check-up, and initially, the checking method was so robust that they put a 4-inch full-length stick in the nose. It was giving more pain than Covid. Long, long queue for testing and without testing certificate, vaccine certificate and registration we cannot fly. The flight tickets were also very costly almost 3-4 times and procedure uploading documents takes double time. Mask and sanitization became routine. Some person could not be recognized due to mask.

There were many waves first, second, third and so on. Mankind learned many lessons from it. In this time of very advanced scientific age also humans became so helpless and craving for medicine and oxygen. India played a very good role in this Covid era by developing and helping and sending Covid vaccine to all countries proving principle of " Vasudhaiva kutumbakam" means world is one family.

Covid gave many negative and positive impression on history of mankind.

Negative were death of family members and suffering of family members were unbearable. Long ques and non-availability of vaccine and medicines. panic environment, lock downs and losing the jobs etc. hotel industry and tourism industry were the worst hit. Doctors were also worst hit and, in some housing society, they were not allowed to enter. I have seen my daughter serving in government hospital with mentally disabled patient it was big challenge for her to control them. Rent of my shop which was given to one restaurant owner slashed to 30% less. Some important project also got delayed in the gulf due to Covid.

Positives were use of money transfer through apps and digital money transfer became worldwide. Some street vendors also started using QR code due to Covid. Digital transaction got maximum boost due to Covid. It made system transparent. Government and people worked together and made some arrangement so that poor people do not suffer. In Bahrain we got vaccination free of cost. Company gave work from home for some time. Some IT companies found work from home so beneficial that they continued work from home and made it permanent even after total covid gone from this world. Covid was game changer for human life.

Chapter

17

Some Lighter Moments

1. One of my expat friends was asking his American boss why he is not sent for foreign tours and training. His boss simply replied him "expat don't expect!"

2. Vasta (personal influence) is a very popular word in the Gulf. Many time vasta makes difference in progress of employee. I told my local friend that now vasta is called "networking" in present world. He laughed and agreed with me.

3. In the gulf if you go to meet in some office and the person whom you went to meet is not in his chair. You ask the person who is sitting beside him "where is this guy? Or has he come today to office? Answer is "he is not my grandfather"!!!

4. In the gulf it happened to me that if I send an email to an engineer of another department for work his autoreply will come "I am on vacation please contact so and so person." I forwarded the email to that second person again, and I received an auto-reply to contact the third person. Again, I sent and thought to meet that third person. When I went to him, his first question was

who told you to contact me? I explained that I received an auto reply from this second person and your name is mentioned in it. He said ok, I will attend, but he has not informed me that he is going on vacation, and I have to take his responsibility!

5. In the gulf I went to attend one meeting. When the whole team arrived, the chairperson started the meeting with "Good morning gentlemen, please give your introduction and tell me how many wives and children you have!"

6. When PM Modi visited Bahrain in August 2019, we went to attend his lecture at a football stadium in Bahrain. On the second day my wife placed a picture of us attending this gathering, in Vadodara SKG society group where we recently shifted. Immediately one phone call came asking: are you in Bahrain? We are also staying in the same society in Vadodara. Then we talked with them. He was a doctor in a Bahrain hospital working as an anaesthetist.

We asked for duplex villa number They replied 47, and ours was 46, so we checked the society map, and to our surprise, we saw they were our neighbours with a common wall. When we met the builder, he was saying one party from Dubai had purchased our next villa, and similarly, when our neighbour was asking about our country, the builder replied that one party from Dubai. So, Bahrain is a very unknown place in India for some people, and we have to tell them that it is near Dubai.!!! Now we became friends in Bahrain due to the Indian PM visit!!!

7. In Yanbu, Saudi Arabia, my friend B was facing a house bug problem too much. He was searching on the internet how to kill them and get rid of them. All pesticides and medicines he experimented with failed. At last, he has done a simple solution. He put all four legs of his cot in water in four small kitchen containers, and that proved right!!!

   We also faced a similar problem when we purchased a second-hand double bed and mattress in Yanbu. At night we felt something biting so kept the light on and searched for the cause. Initially I didn't find anything but again something bites and we just lifted the mattress and found a large number of house bugs. Second day we dismantled the double bed and put it on the terrace under direct sunlight so that all bugs can be killed.

8. One of my Arabic friends in Saudi Arabia told me, "I don't know why Indian restaurants are not taking my delivery order." I said what you told them. He said, "I want to order food?" The receptionist asked my name, and I said, "NAHI" he put down my phone. Then I

explained to him that in Hindi/Urdu, NAHI means no name. so that is why they put your phone down!!! Actually, NAHI is a name in Arabic. Other surnames or family names are AL SEHERI, ALGHAMDI, AL BANDAR, Qahtani, Almutawa, etc. Some surnames in Bahrain are from villages like Sitrawi, Muharaqi, and Ekri, etc.

9. In the gulf One friend, R, was driving his car after drinking. One local person hit his car with my friend's car. A local person offered to settle outside without going to the police. My friend insisted on going to the police. When they went to the police, the police got a doubt on my friend and tested for alcohol. And he was found drunk, so they put him in jail. From jail, he rang another friend and his boss. They tried to get him out of jail. Police presented him to court the next day. Somehow a judge looking at his age pardoned him as he was looking very young. But told his boss to take care of his son properly. Don't allow him to make this mistake again! His boss said OK Sir. The next day, my friend R was sharing his experience and said morning breakfast in jail was very good!

10. During my visit to Dubai from KSA for official tour I went to one factory in Jabel Ali for inspection of heat exchanger. I told one of workshop supervisor that I am coming from Al Jubail KSA. He said sir I was in Saudi. In Saudi you can do three things only. Eat Sleep Work,

Eat Sleep Work, Eat Sleep Work. He told this with so much emotion and breathlessly that I thought he must be fully frustrated in Saudi!!

11. One of my friends went for open heart surgery in India and had taken one-year medical leave. After coming back from vacation, he went to bank to withdraw money. He asked bank officer he want to withdraw money after showing his bank account proof. Bank officer said your money is transferred to kings account. He thought bank officer is making joke. He again asked what? yes, your money is transferred to kings account you have to do certain procedure to get it back! It is rules in KSA if you do not operate bank account for more than six months, money gets transferred to kings account.

12. One oil and gas company from gulf came for walk in interview at Mumbai. When they saw CV of candidate's, designation mentioned was deputy general manager and general manager in the CV. One of officer came out side and announced that they came for recruitment of engineers only and not general managers! So, whoever want to get DGM and GM post they can go home. Actually, private sector oil and gas company have made inflation of designation. They removed designation as engineer, they started from manager designation and then senior manager, DGM and GM. Worldwide there are only few GM in a company but in

India if you go to those oil and gas companies there are 300 DGM and 200 GM!

13. From one oil and gas company of gulf some general managers were sent for foreign training in Europe. They were provided female secretaries to help. When they came back to gulf, all got married with secretaries and came back with new brides!

Chapter

18

Some Sad Moments

In the gulf all days are not the same and sometimes some incident happens which reminds us how temporary our life is. We try to plan so many things but in a minute it becomes uncertain.

1. When I was in Saudi Yanbu, one of my friend's daughters were in India. They wanted to come to visit Saudi during their vacation. His brother and friend came by car to drop them off at Ahmedabad airport at night and returned after dropping them. While returning by car, they met with an accident and died on the spot. Actually, the truck was parked on the side of the road without any indication during night, and their car plunged inside the truck from the backside. These are very common type of accident on the highways in India.

2. When I was in Yanbu, a new petrochemical company project was started, and many Indians from my ex-company were recruited as plant operators, engineers and technicians. One engineer, Mr M, was having a very sad story. He was working in Saudi and his two sons were travelling to Saudi from New Delhi airport.

While taking off, the plane caught fire and, in that fire, his two sons died along with other passengers. They were crying as told by my friend. Now, only Mr. and Mrs were staying in Saudi Arabia. They were once travelling in a car with his friend's family, in from Riyadh to Dammam and met with a road accident, his wife and his friend and friend's wife died. He was the only survivor. He went back and decided not to come back to Saudi Arabia again. Now in a new company, he arrived with his new wife as he married again. So, life has endless possibilities. Never lose hope. Keep going.

3. When I was in Al Jubail, one of my friend's wife, was going back to India with some other family. On the way from AL Jubail to Dammam airport, their car overturned, and his wife got a head injury and died. It was very shocking news for him. Taking dead body to India is also a big project in gulf as procedure itself takes half to one month.

4. When I was in Bahrain, my younger brother called me to tell me that my niece, Yashu daughter of my middle brother Shashi met with a road accident and was seriously injured and in hospital at Vadodara. I got a heavy shock and could not do anything for a moment. I immediately informed my friend and department head that we had to go immediately. My friend helped me to book air ticket for me and my wife, and we went by

night flight. In the morning, we reached Vadodara, my city. We lost her next day, and that incident became very difficult to withstand for our family. Still her face comes to my mind and I become thought less.

5. During Covid, some of my friends' fathers and mothers died, and they could not go to India to attend their funerals. One of my friends lost a job due to Covid 19.

Chapter

19

Conclusion

1. Prepare yourself for gulf jobs though internet surfing, networking and attending interviews.

2. Prepare mind set for global citizen and remove all type stigma and of mental blocks and treat everybody equal without biased based on caste, creed, race, religion, color, country and gender.

3. Practice leaving alone without family for some time before going to gulf.

4. Learn 3C i.e. car, computer and cooking.

5. Risk is everywhere, risk cannot be eliminated but it can be mitigated. Always have plan B.

6. Formula for success in life is equal to 50 percent intelligence and 50 percent daring.

7. Have a hobby in life so that in the time of loneliness you can cultivate it and enjoy.

8. Never give up hope. Keep on giving interviews one day it will click and you will be in the gulf.

9. Stay minimum for 3 months after arriving in the gulf.

Don't make hurry for going back to India. Culture shock is normal.

10. Do SWOT analysis of self before landing at gulf.

11. Be proactive and change job and country at every five year interval.